What Is Jiu Jitsu?

The Martial Arts and How to Understand Them

D. S. Hopkins

What Is Jiu Jitsu?
The Martial Arts and How to Understand Them
Copyright ©2015 D. S. Hopkins

ISBN 978-1506-912-93-6 PBK
ISBN 978-1506-900-03-2 EBK

September 2020

Published and Distributed by
First Edition Design Publishing, Inc.
Sarasota, FL USA
www.firsteditiondesignpublishing.com

Text, Illustrations and Photos by D.S. Hopkins

Disclaimer

Not the author, nor the publisher, or anyone else assumes any responsibility for the use or misuse or application of any knowledge contained within this book. The information founder herein, textual or illustrative, is for academic purposes only and not intended for usage in any instructional capacity and should not be attempted. Any martial art practice should only be exercised under the instruction of qualified persons that are capable of providing appropriate training.

Any references to persons having the same or similar names is purely coincidental.

For my mom and sister.
Thinking of their well-being. Always.

Acknowledgments

The author would like to express genuine gratitude to Jehovah, the Lord Christ Jesus, and the Holy Ghost, without whose intervention something very dark and different would have been written.

The author would also like to extend gratitude to M. Kennedy, without whom this would have been far more difficult to piece together.

Table of Contents

Preface

It's not uncommon to take for granted the things we've acquired expertise in, especially when we have a duration of experience that has grown to be so natural and a part of us that we no longer register it as anything but ordinary. The truth is though that it's only really *ordinary* to us, these subjects we've become informed on or skills we've developed, and we sometimes might find ourselves assuming that what we have to offer isn't anything that the next person doesn't know or can't do. As a martial artist I've caught myself doing this repeatedly over the years, sometimes aloud, sometimes in silence, but making this erroneous assumption regardless, which inadvertently devalues oneself in the process. It doesn't always occur to the person speaking or teaching or writing just exactly how much they have to offer those who are searching for answers. Now that I've experienced this jolt a number of times, I find myself more wary of it and less likely to let it pass unchecked. But it's not until one actually hears the kind of inquiries being made by other people that the thought begins to take shape that the world has far more question marks in it than answers – answers that we, our unremarkable selves, may happen to have.

I began the study of Jūjutsu in 1994. I never thought once back then that I'd continue and continue and continue until I was writing a work such as this. *C'est la vie*, as the French say, *that's life*. My earliest experiences with the martial arts go back to 1986, then again in 1990, but it wasn't until 1994 that I began a serious study, nor was that study limited just to Jūjutsu. I eventually experimented with *Tangsoodo*, a Korean striking system (made famous by Chuck Norris), then to *Aikido* (made famous by Steven Seagal), and even developed an interest in *Aiki-Jūjutsu* due to the interest in Aikido and then eventually came full circle back to Jūjutsu. For now I'll only say that my original intentions, all those years ago, had been to eventually write something more exhaustive...something masterful; a real contribution to modern hand-to-hand and one that used Jūjutsu as its foundational experience.

And that still isn't without possibility. But I think now, looking at the wide range of misunderstanding and general lack of information among most people, that what really needs to precede anything so complex is a far lighter work with 'what is' and 'how to' and 'where from' as its main governing themes. In this brief book I've tried to keep things as simplified and streamlined as possible and written it for the layman and not the initiated. I've built the architecture of the book around the question *"What Is Jiu Jitsu?"* and from there branched out to a broad and general treatment of the martial sciences. There are nine chapters with the first four more centered on Jūjutsu than say the far more generalized chapters that immediately succeed

1

them. The book then returns to Jūjutsu in chapter 7 and again in chapter 9. The reason I've written wide sections of this book on martial arts as opposed to Jūjutsu specifically is that it would have been something of a squandered opportunity to write it without at least touching on the broader view: most martial arts work on exactly the same principles, only using different substance. It was a chance in chapters five and six, and again at eight, to stretch out and give the reader a chance to apply an analytical eye to the martial sciences in general, and use a form of metric that could perhaps be used universally across the greater spectrum to get a feel for the entire picture, not just a part of it.

I think it's fair to say that Jūjutsu is the focus even when it's not. And what I mean is that it forms the underlying foundation of this writer's experience, and though not strictly limited to it, it is the far greater part of where my understanding developed. So even when not making direct reference to it, the reader may assume that many conclusions are drawn from Jūjutsu first and foremost, and other disciplines afterward, whether they be Japanese grappling or Korean striking arts. The reader will encounter specific terms I use to categorize like *Minimal, Chain* or *Variable* and *Common, Weaponized* and *Specialized*. These are created for the sake of organizational structure, and to my knowledge have no origin or similar usage outside the context of their usage here. In select places I will use Japanese terminology, and while this means little or nothing to the reader uninitiated in the martial arts, to anyone else I'd say that these don't always align to what is currently the accepted nomenclature within the mainstream Jūjutsu, Aiki-Jūjutsu, Judo or Aikido disciplines and their respective governing bodies. I do appreciate that not everyone who reads what I have to say here, the conclusions I propound, or the encompassing view I take of the martial arts and the governing rules that I apply across the whole of them, will share the same feelings or outlook – they may even quite plainly dislike it. To them I say here and now that these views are sincerely mine, and I am every bit entitled to them as they are to theirs, but I still hope that such readers will come away with some wholesome benefit for having read the book – and if they don't....well, *c'est la vie.*

The ninth and final chapter is a short look at three techniques from the system of Jūjutsu being referenced here. The reader is given a small idea of the kind of combative engagements these techniques try to create and control. It shows generally where the focus of the Jūjutsu martial art is in terms of its grappling tactics. In the same chapter I've also made sure that the three techniques being used purposely demonstrates something of the character of the three major types of Jūjutsu in an attempt to give the reader a clear impression of the potential differences. Here then begins the answer to *"What Is Jiu Jitsu?"* And the larger explanation of *The Martial Arts and How To Understand Them.*

Pronunciation

I notice you say Jūjutsu, and not Jiu Jitsu. Why is that?
Because Jūjutsu is how the Japanese say it. Jiu Jitsu is not.
But everyone says Jiu Jitsu, and no one says Jūjutsu.
That makes 'Jiu Jitsu' acceptable, it doesn't make it accurate.

Jūjutsu is Jiu Jitsu is Jujitsu. They're all the same thing, just differently spelled and pronounced. The term Jiu Jitsu, as well as Jujitsu, are accepted pronunciations and spellings in many western countries, but possess no concurrence in Japanese: that means that if you were to say the word aloud to them in their own language they'd either not understand what you were saying, or if they did it would only be due to having heard western media mispronounce it so often. When *Kanji* (the Japanese writing system) is translated into English (or the Latin alphabet) it should see the word written and spelled like this: Jūjutsu. Since the inception of Japanese martial arts into the West the pronunciation and spelling were for a long time, and for the most part remain, Jiu Jitsu. It's literally been in use so long it's accepted as correct, even though from a linguistic and cultural perspective it is an inaccuracy. I say inaccurate as opposed to wrong, because the word 'wrong' – though it's technically correct – feels a little too strong for the discrepancy it describes, especially when the population at large were introduced to the current term from the beginning and have never been informed as to the differences and details.

So, is it wrong to say Jiu Jitsu instead of Jūjutsu? No, of course not, but I do think it would be wrong for me not to express this truth when so very few are aware of it. And I especially think that we as students (as we all are, whether it be with two years practice, ten years or twenty, of martial arts or of another culture) should at the very least be conscious of the finer details, of what makes one thing linguistically and historically and culturally true, and what makes another thing *almost* true. Both may very well be acceptable in common usage, and in this case Jiu Jitsu is more used and understood than Jūjutsu, but for the sake of promoting professionalism and culture, we should all know the difference. There is a certain scholastic standard that shouldn't only be sought for, but attained, and then maintained; an awareness of the minutia, consequential or not, is what sets those who strive for a scholarly standard apart from everyone else. The name of a thing, its designation as assigned by those who conceived it, may seem like something less important than the substance of the thing itself, but that's hard to imagine given that the name embodies what it is, far more than any component part. The study of an art should begin with knowing its proper name (even if it has fallen out of favor) - it'd be nothing but professional for each of us to do that. There is also a certain necessary respect and honor that is rightly bestowed on those to whom these arts firstly belong when we speak their words the way they do – it'd be nothing but cultured for each of us to do that.

Jūjutsu

柔術

Jūjutsu is a word composed of dual terms, and these two terms are represented by the words *Ju* and *Jutsu*: Ju means soft or gentle in the Japanese tongue, while Jutsu could be translated as skill or art. The concept created then by combining these two words is something approximating *Soft Skill* or *Gentle Art*.

With Jūjutsu defined and given meaning we can turn our attention to the next most relevant word we need translated - *Aiki*: in reference to Aiki-Jūjutsu, the sister discipline of Jūjutsu. Aiki could be interpreted like this: *Ai* could translate as harmony or harmonized, and *Ki* could mean spirit or power, so that the term Aiki would read in English as Harmonized Power. In totality the designation Aiki-Jūjutsu would translate literally as Harmonized Power of the Gentle Art. The reasoning for this suffix of Aiki is that philosophically the discipline attempts to move in harmony with the attacker, never against him, and this ideal is the defining characteristic of the martial art.

The reason for the need to interpret Aiki-Jūjutsu as well as Jūjutsu itself for the reader is due to the relevance the former has when discussing the latter: these two disciplines share much common history and an intrinsic relationship, having far more similarities than differences. In the following chapter these terms will be revisited and made clear as to their philosophical impacts on the fight systems to which they belong.

Chapter 1

Modes of Jūjutsu: The Ancient and Modern

When considering martial arts, it has become commonplace to categorize them into two separate species: grappling and striking. This is the most basic generalization that can be made regarding the archaic combat sciences. A striking art attacks its enemy using repeated and rapidly varying combinations of hits: punches, kicks, knees, elbows, chops, ridge hands, reverse chops etc., which all make vicious and efficient use of blunt force trauma to destroy a threat. Boxing, Karate, *Taekwondo*, *Kung Fu*, *Muay Thai*, Kick Boxing and *Savate* all represent types of striking arts. Grappling arts attack using throws, sweeps, balance breakers, locks, torques and chokes usually in sustained contact (a firm hold that remains unbroken) to destroy the threat through bone breaking, asphyxiation, joint stress or the blunt force from ground-impact as a result of being thrown.

Weaponized martial arts are often considered in a category of their own. In many forms of Jūjutsu and her offspring, however, the relationship to weaponry is so integral that divorce should be all but impossible. This intimacy with weaponized combat is also prevalent in Karate and Ninjutsu, among others.

Jūjutsu is almost unanimously regarded as a grappling art. For the *most* part this is true. The greater majority of its maneuvers make use of grappling principles in the way of throws, joint-manipulation, sweeps and choke holds. Yet there is not an inconsiderable number of techniques that entail the skilled usage of blunt force strikes – whether it be delivered by hand, foot, shin, elbow, knee, fingers or otherwise - to achieve combat objectives. It's quite common, even expected, for a Jūjutsu maneuver to end, or have executed somewhere within the order of operations, a violent trauma or crush or fracture by way of skilled and calculated striking principles. That being said the degree of striking that most Jūjutsu systems use is vastly outweighed by the grappling principles. Also, and often not considered at all, is the truth of Jūjutsu's relationship with the Japanese sword – the *katana*. Most modes of Jūjutsu will have some curriculum, even a small one, that honor the practice of *Iaido* or *Iaijutsu*, the art of drawing the sword, or of *Kendo* or *Kenjutsu* – the way of the sword.

The way that Jūjutsu is being presented here thus far probably doesn't align that well to the popular view that has grown up around the discipline. It's easy to understand the source of the confusion however, given that some of the later modes of Jūjutsu, particularly Judo and its focus on the take-downs and the ground-control aspects of Jūjutsu, creates an almost signature appearance in the way its adherents grapple one another on the mats. Even more outstanding in uniqueness of style though is Brazilian Jiu Jitsu, which drew so much of its early inspiration from Judo, but has since elaborated on its anatomical mechanics with something of an ultra-focus, a trait that has allowed it to achieve unprecedented successes in close-quarter fighting from the horizontal position. The Brazilian model of Jūjutsu, however, represents a fundamental shift away from the archetypes that gave birth to it; the word archetype being used here to identify those first colossi that lived and breathed on the battlefields of medieval Japan, an environment that required something far less specialized and far more versatile. But it is, in fact, due to this peculiarity of specialization and all the attendant successes resultant of that specialization, it has become one of the foremost sought-after disciplines in the world, and has identified Brazil as its cradle of conception.

Even within the narrow confines of the discipline of Jūjutsu itself – setting Aiki-Jūjutsu, Judo, Aikido and Brazilian Jiu Jitsu quite apart from it – and considering only the archetype, Japanese Jūjutsu, alone, we see that the martial art exists in a state of varying conditions. These conditions can be simplified down to *two* for the sake of discussion. The first condition we find the martial art in is one that creates a form of Jūjutsu that is much closer to its medieval predecessor in material, outlook and design than the other. This is a defining trait which makes it more faithful to its origins. The second condition we find Jūjutsu in is one shifted toward a design to better answer these later-day combat challenges occurring in the modern world (many of these challenges also take place in cultures alien to that environment where the martial art was originally intended to perform). These traits make it more tactically viable and valuable to its adherents. In both instances they have roughly the same substance, or rather technical resources, but exist in different arrangement with different focus. The comparison then is one of purpose as opposed to essence. Even with the difference in the way the material is allotted and tailored throughout the two models, the modernized variant still bears a resemblance to the feudal mode of Jūjutsu that was practiced in pre-industrial Japan (which is to say before the advent of Judo or the exportation of Jūjutsu to the wider world). It is this later heavily modernized variant the reader is most likely to see. The earlier, largely unaltered form is something of a rarity by comparison.

Sisters: Jūjutsu and Aiki-Jūjutsu

The parentage of all modern Jūjutsu systems can be traced back to two methods, one more famous and one less so: Jūjutsu and Aiki-Jūjutsu. To the untrained eye these two sister arts appear nearly identical in writing, and indeed they share more similarities than differences. Despite how closely related they are, have significantly different approaches to combat.

The reader must here understand a few fundamental truths concerning Jūjutsu systems. Most of the classical modes and the modern variants that came afterwards (classical systems of Jūjutsu are those most closely related to their medieval forerunners) have within them an arsenal, or a small and limited set, of striking tactics. These usually, but not always, include finger strikes, front kicks, side kicks, push kicks, round kicks, punches, chops, reverse chops, back fists, elbows, knees and so on. That short list appears more robust when it's written than it actually is, but compared to the martial arts that are actually of the striking species it is tiny and simplistic.

Not only are the striking assets within Jūjutsu systems limited in number, but worse is their deficiency in fluid application; fluid meaning the ability to strike and maintain an ongoing, variable pattern of methodical but unpredictable attack. In layman's terms, this system of fight simply isn't meant to 'spar' the way one would expect a *Subumnim* of Tangsoodo or a *Shihan* of Karate or a Golden Gloves Boxer to spar. Sparring is of course practiced in many schools that study traditional Jūjutsu, and it absolutely should be, but it's clear to the analytical eye that the striking instruments in this system are clearly designed to function in support of grappling methodology. Throughout the course of a combative engagement, opportunities present themselves at odd and even unpredictable moments. A throat happens to be unprotected, or a jugular, or the cervical vertebrae, or an eye...but without the right tool at the right instant decisive advantages cannot be capitalized upon. It really is quite sobering to begin an intensive study of Jūjutsu and realize just how often these vulnerabilities present themselves, not only in our training partner's defenses, but also in our own. There is no better way to sharpen and tighten the defenses against future opponents by defending your weaknesses from a training partner in the present; someone mock-attacking with highly effective combat skills.

The deceptive value also can't be overstated: a feinted front kick can drop someone's defenses and allow a clinch on the upper body, at the collar or elbows for example, or a knee executed while in a static, unmoving position can force the other to alter his posture for the sake of protection, creating a new position to the advantage of the initiator. These are all time honored tactics and should be practiced every bit as diligently as the grappling maneuvers they support.

Alternatively, the study of most classical striking disciplines, such as Karate or Tangsoodo, will yield the same analysis with reverse values: a small arsenal of grappling tactics will exist within a complex striking methodology, limited and deficient, but present and placed there particularly for the express purpose of supporting a larger striking-based strategy. To have such an inclusion of inconsistent material, grappling within striking or striking within grappling, isn't in my estimation a bad policy, even if it is only of marginal value when compared to the system's focused architecture. It could be argued, and not in vain, that the presence of tactics so foreign to the nature of a fight system can only create an appreciation for whatever species of fight those handful of tactics represent. Regardless of whatever discipline is being practiced, a healthy respect for everything unknown should always be maintained.

It was this very experience that pushed this writer towards Tangsoodo, a sister of Taekwondo, which are both striking disciplines of Korean origin. What became plainly apparent in such a venture was that by having some small minority of maneuvers not congruent or common with the martial art being used (like the striking tactics within Jūjutsu for example), the practitioner was pushed to explore more complete and thorough striking strategies and by doing so caused an initially lop-sided skill set to better balance out and diversify.

It wouldn't be an exaggeration, nor outside the bounds of what is currently observable in the more traditionally-aligned Jūjutsu systems, to quantify as much as ten to fifteen percent of the architecture as striking tactics. These striking tools are carefully situated within the system to increase the combat effectiveness of the maneuvers, to assist in providing a closing move, or at other times an opening move. The 'Ground and Pound' tactics that emerged in the Mixed Martial Arts (MMA) certainly demonstrate an example of this: grappling tactics that allow a fighter to control an opponent, and striking tactics that allow the fighter to strike him while such control is being exercised. While fifteen percent represents a not insignificant measure of striking content in a highly classical Jūjutsu system, it must be stated that this is the very most that one could expect to find in such methods of fight. The percentage would be considerably less within the younger modes of Jūjutsu and of varying quantity throughout all the others depending on their modernization. Some Brazilian systems might have as little as five to ten percent, while a modernized Jūjutsu or Aiki-Jūjutsu system might have anything between ten and fifteen percent, and Judo would be close to nil.

The last advantage, and certainly not the least, to having such striking material made a part of a predominantly grappling system, would be the expertise that would develop applying counter measures to the striking attacks themselves. After all, to defend oneself against something one must first understand it, and there would be no better way to do that than to practice with it. This would be especially true if the striking tactics being practiced were in wide service and expected to be encountered amongst one's adversaries.

This hopefully clarifies the relative amount of striking skills that are likely to be found in various modes of Jūjutsu. Yet, the commonality doesn't end there, as various modes of Jūjutsu also share many of the same locks, throws, torques and chokes. These in many cases are applied in a similar manner against the same attacks. It's not uncommon to go from school to school and find common throws or sweeps or balance breakers with little or no variation. Other times you could visit three different schools that claim to have descended from the same tradition (same root) and have unusually different answers to the same attack, and all positioned at disparate ranks. This happens, and with utterly casual regularity. It's chiefly due to the fact that many masters and grand masters reallocate tactics and maneuvers to what they feel are more appropriate positions in the systems they use. They then teach the system after its reconfiguration, passing it on in its modified format, and this becomes the new standard for that particular school. It may also be that the techniques themselves will bear designations not in sync with other schools of the same discipline, yet the maneuver is done precisely the same. In other cases the maneuver may be different as well, for better or for worse. All of this is to be expected.

To help the reader better appreciate the discussions later in this book concerning Jūjutsu and her relatives, a brief look at her sister, Aiki-Jūjutsu, is first required; to highlight all the philosophical traits of Aiki-Jūjutsu is to equally highlight what Jūjutsu for the most part isn't. The closeness of these two archetype systems in origin, aims and their technical approach to attack and defense, is so very similar that they at once appear more sisterly than estranged to the untrained observer or uninitiated student. And as already said they are in fact closer than farther apart in conception and construction. The true fork of what otherwise would have been a rough parallel path of existence and development is delineated by where each discipline has placed emphasis concerning combat doctrine.

The key difference between the two is for the most part philosophical in nature: Jūjutsu, through employment of various techniques, is designed to use an adversary's exertions against him by countering with moves and maneuvers that capitalize upon the very way he is attacking. It does this by way of critical striking, sweeps, throws, chokes and joint-locks. Aiki-Jūjutsu does this as well, but with more of an unconventional outlook: its primary goal isn't completely combative, but rather universal. What this means is that the philosophy of the discipline, which on the broadest basis is an aspiration to move harmonically with the universe and all existence, sees the assailant as a force that needs to be balanced which is accomplished through blending. To this end the system has been technically designed to reflect this philosophy by the way it accepts and meshes with the attacking force, never offering direct opposition or friction, and by doing so moves in ideal unison with the attacker's energy, letting it provide the power with which it will be brought to stillness. This mentality creates a mindset of accepting momentum, never countering it, but absorbing it. All of its techniques attempt to make use of it and continually redirect the output of the enemy in a way that assists the counter move that the Aiki-Jūjutsu system wants to reply with.

In contrast to Jūjutsu, Aiki-Jūjutsu is found to be narrower in scope of application, but due to its intricacy it requires sharper execution. Owing to its origins and closer relationship with Kenjutsu, the art of the sword, the lineage it shares with the *katana* can still be seen in its maneuvers. Most of its techniques reflect the swordsman's mentality of optimum operational distance to be close enough to acquire bone locks and joint-throws, but far enough to control the pace and character of the conflict. Like its sister, Jūjutsu, it seeks to manipulate and so dictate the terms of the engagement – this includes how to manage distance, open it and remove it. Many of its moves come from before 1868 A.D. when fencing was still common in the island nation, and being as such is replete with those counter-moves that protect the sword, thwart any attempts to disarm it, and fight with the same rapid engage-and-neutralize decisiveness in its absence. Stated like this it's not difficult for the reader to imagine that Aiki-Jūjutsu is a system of fight more utilized from the position of standing on the feet or from sitting on them (as in the *seiza* posture, or sitting position), than, say, from positions that are horizontally-situated, though these types of techniques do exist in sparse numbers.

This preferred 'upright' or 'feet first' posture has not only been influenced by the Japanese sword arts, but is also compounded by a combat philosophy steeped in a mysticism that strives to express physically what it believes spiritually – that the energy of the attacker, like the physical assault itself, must be blended with to be truly overcome. This martial art is founded upon the ideology of blending. In physical practice this translates into *reaction*, given that in order to use the discipline's harmonizing principles there must first be some attack to harmonize with; if one does not initiate attack but only reacts to it then the system is counter-offensive. This blending of the martial artist with the attack of the assailant is for the most part accomplished through interception and redirection – and what is most noteworthy here is the approach to how such a martial artist is required to move and engage.

To serve this principle of harmonization meticulous footwork, deft deflections and precise clinches of hostile limbs are required as well as the dexterity to produce cunning locks while in motion with a resistant foe - which in turn all demands a surpassing *mobility*. Thus the tactics almost always keep the practitioner on his feet for those very attributes of speed and maneuverability that only a vertical posture can deliver and his system of fight so deeply depends on. Also, not unlike what is typically experienced in sword dueling, is the need to engage, disengage and reengage rapidly, and at will, with multiple opponents. Aiki-Jūjutsu will always attempt, like Aikido its offspring, to actuate its throws, locks and holds from the vertical position, while still standing. This may be one of the greatest differences between it and its sister art, Jūjutsu. While Jūjutsu does this as well, attempting control and lockup of an opponent from the vertical position, it doesn't focus on it nearly as heavily.

One need only observe all these traits in Aikido, Aiki-Jūjutsu's offspring, to see them emphasized in the descendent-system and so also made more conspicuous in the parent-system. Aikido is the product of Aiki-Jūjutsu, even as Judo is the product of Jūjutsu. *Aikidoka*, the students and teachers of Aikido, are continually in a state of mind to redirect attack, and to accomplish this they have a wondrous array of displacements, deflections and holds designed to make use of the way their enemy moves. Like *Jigoro Kano's* redesign of Jūjutsu to produce Judo, *Morehei Uesheiba*, Aikido's founder, redesigned Aiki-Jūjutsu to suit his new vision of it. This was considerably less aggressive in posture and more fluid and polished, but never lost that signature nimbleness of foot or deftness of hand that Aiki-Jūjutsu was identified for. Oft times Aikido is represented more as a mystical art than a martial one; however, not all masters or grand masters of that discipline promote it as such and there is some degree of division. The martial arts film star Steven Seagal did much to popularize a very combative and very physical form of Aikido, making a tremendous statement that the discipline wasn't necessarily bound to a prescribed use one way or the other, but could be used in the way that suited its practitioner best. He painted a very effective and impressive view of the discipline's potential.

For this reason Aiki-Jūjutsu students and masters and grand masters are very nearly almost always on their feet, or if not then their knees. This practical truth concerning the vertical posturing and the execution of techniques from the feet and knees may seem unnatural to those who are unfamiliar with the origins of these fight systems, but the reader must remember that these were made to be used militarily, on battlefields. Out there in the blood and muck and chaos it was almost infinitely more natural to fight upright than on the ground as weapons of war such as sword and spear and bow, *ken* and *yari* and *kyu*, were used when standing. If there was occasion to go so low to the ground as to lay on it, this was usually due to blood loss and imminent death.

These then are the two major defining forces of the Aiki-Jūjutsu tradition: firstly, its conceptional birthplace being so related to the sword arts; and secondly, a philosophy which is typified by exemplary footwork and precision redirection that create a signature look and feel and battlefield efficacy that the discipline had once become famous for.

While so many of the technical principles between Jūjutsu and Aiki-Jūjutsu are identical, the actual employment of those principles in their maneuvers is where the two vary and stray apart: Jūjutsu's policy of directness – utilizing a route of attack as short and economical as may be –

allows for a wider and more versatile system, making up what it loses in elegance of principle with aggressiveness and efficiency. It at once seems to have more practicality across a broader spectrum while Aiki-Jūjutsu strives for something loftier, displaying a refinement in line with its reach for a universal experience. The more obvious lines of attack that Jūjutsu takes advantage of and the ground mechanics it embraces, combined with the maneuvers it shares with Aiki-Jūjutsu, make it more attractive to the combatant burdened by all the grim possibilities that physicality will allow.

The real significant deviation in physical details of technique between one system and the other are 'how' the maneuvers are realized. Aiki-Jūjutsu's maneuvers are closely modeled to function on joint-manipulation; it attacks the body's ranges of motion to actuate nearly all its balance breakers, joint-locks, joint-throws and escapes. And though its choke holds, sweeps and strikes stand apart from using joint manipulation, they do represent the smaller part of the system's arsenal.

Throughout this text some terminology is used frequently to identify maneuvers, holds or people that could seem confusing to the new student or reader. This is particularly true during the picture sets that outline the transition of movements within a maneuver, and in such cases where a recurring terminology is being used (the term in question will have its English translation next to it in brackets). The person performing the maneuver is often referred to as *tori (pronounced tore-ee)*, who is the person under attack or completing the technique; the person performing the attack is often referred to as *uke (pronounced ou-kay)*, who will be the person being thrown.

Below follows two examples that clearly demonstrate the difference with which these two disciplines will answer the same attacks. In both examples the types of attacks that are being used are of the *common* variety (common as in they are readily encountered in any number of places). The first attack is a bear-hug from the back that does not pin the arms within the encircling hug, while the second is a wrist hold where the attacker clasps each wrist of the defender. With these two maneuvers we begin to see the characteristics of each discipline, Jūjutsu and Aiki-Jūjutsu, as discussed above.

In the first set we see the attacker (uke) has begun the bear hug from the back, or blindside of the defender (tori), and the defense that will be used is a small joint lock of the finger that allows tori to escape the bear hug, and pivot to create a larger lock called *Sank-jo* (pronounced *Sawn-Kee-Oh*). This is the type of counter move one might see from a more contemporary and less traditional Aiki-Jūjutsu student.

Fig 1.0, as said, sees the attack beginning.

Fig 1.0

In Fig 1.1 the defender begins to search for the clasp of their attacker's hands. This clasp is usually a type of grip nothing more complicated than a person's hand tightly grasping their opposite wrist, creating a simple 'overhand grip'. The defender is searching for the hand that is actually doing the gripping, as any one of those fingers can be 'peeled' back if our own finger tips can get underneath (an easy thing to do).

Fig 1.1

Fig 1.2 will give the reader an impression of what was meant by one hand clasping the other hand in an overhand grip.

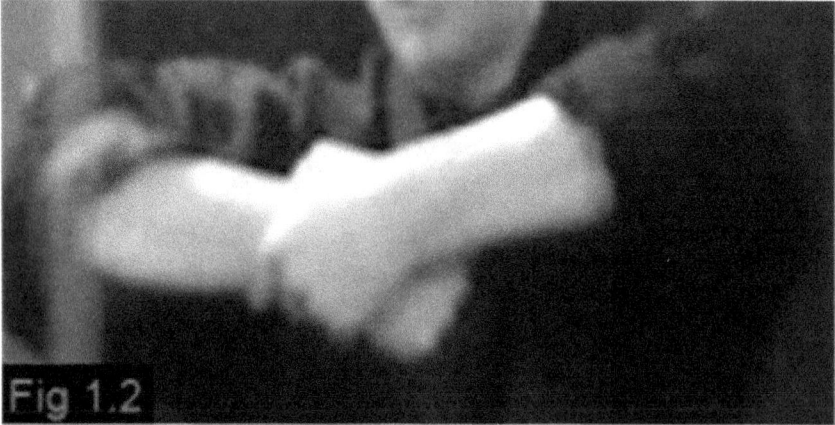

Fig 1.2

In Fig 1.3 the defender has managed to pry one of the clasping fingers free and is now in the process of wrenching it off and away from the body (the small inset picture in the lower right hand of Fig 1.3 depicts the direction it is moving).

Fig 1.3

Fig 1.4 sees the attacker letting go as the finger has been cranked beyond its range of motion and the associated pain has necessitated a release of the grip. Tori moves in the direction of the arrows, his direction reinforcing the hyper extension of the finger.

Fig 1.4

Fig 1.5 makes visible the Aiki-Jūjutsu policy of achieving the most effect with the smallest exertions, as well as the philosophy of using bodily motion and position to assist if not entirely complete the joint manipulation. Here merely turning the anatomy in a tight circle creates a pain great enough to begin a crumpling effect on the attacker (uke), and their anatomy now follows the direction of the pain being inflicted.

Fig 1.5

Fig 1.6 to Fig 1.7 are the transition from the finger lock to a larger joint lock of the wrist, one sometimes referred to as Sank-jo (the third principle in Aikido and Aiki-Jūjutsu; and spelled with the Latin alphabet also *Sankyo* and *Sankjo*). As tori continues to turn around while hyper-extending first the finger, now torquing the wrist, the pain increases with the movement of his body's rotation toward the attacker.

Fig 1.6

The larger circle atop the photo in Fig 1.7 shows the direction in which tori is turning, while the smaller circle shows the direction in which tori is beginning to torque the wrist of uke. The opposing directions contribute to a torsion effect. In the lower right of the picture is the inset of the hand and the direction the fingers are being bent in; here, however, the picture of the hand has been turned to reflect how uke's hand is actually situated in the larger picture – which is palm down and the fingers pointing back towards himself.

Fig 1.7

Fig 2.0 begins at the beginning of the bear hug attack again, but with one difference: now tori, the defender, will use a common defense of Jūjutsu to defeat the attack, one that seeks to use the principles of lift to disrupt and break balance.

Fig 2.0

Fig 2.1 shows tori stepping wide (similar to a straddle leg stance and according to the space covered by the arrow) and dropping his own center of gravity to help thwart any attempt by uke to pick him up, but foremost to achieve necessary positioning to execute his counter move.

Fig 2.1

Fig 2.2 sees the beginning of the execution of the counter move. Tori (defender) reaches for the attacker's (or uke's) near leg which is now directly between his own due to the step he's made.

Fig 2.2

Fig 2.3 shows tori attaining a hold around the ankle area, cupping it firmly with both hands. In a combative engagement even a handful of fabric close to the attacker's foot would be enough as long as it didn't tear or give way.

Fig 2.3

Fig 2.4 sees the attacker (uke) falling fast with broken balance. Tori (defender) has not only pulled his leg out from underneath him, but also has used his own buttocks or pelvis to lock the attacker's knee by forcing downward as the hands pull the ankle up. Even without the knee locked, and only the downward force of tori's hips against the leg, it is often enough to complete the maneuver.

Fig 2.4

Fig 2.5 leaves tori in position with multiple options for continuance, anything from twisting uke over to his stomach and choke-hunting, to locking the leg outright to assuming full mount.

Fig 2.5

Hopefully the reader can gain the first insight from this comparison to begin to understand the divergence in method between these two systems of fight: Aiki-Jūjutsu's focus on joints and how position empowers the manipulation of them to greater and greater locks, and Jūjutsu's focus on lift and balance, seeking to secure better and better positions.

The second example in this photo set is even simpler. This example makes use of a beginner position, and what is also a rudimentary common attack: the double wrist grab, or two hands clasping two wrists.

It is a very basic attempt at controlling someone else by holding them firmly at the wrists. There is a greater degree of subtlety here, and is hard to depict without using a great many more photographs and ones of much higher quality, but hopefully these will suffice.

Fig 3.0 of the following sequence sees an Aiki-Jūjutsu approach; a throw sometimes referred to as *tenshi nage*, or heaven and earth throw. Tori will rotate his hands so that the palm of the near hand rises between uke's arms skyward, and the other faces out and earthward.

Fig 3.0

Fig 3.1 has the defender, tori, raise his right hand palm upward to the sky, turning his own wrist within the attacker's grip. His left hand makes the same movement within the hand holding it but with the palm pointing earthward toward the floor (note the direction of the arrows). Tori's far-side leg has advanced a step toward uke here.

Fig 3.1

Fig 3.2 shows tori having stepped forward and to the outside of uke a little, his far hand still pointing downward, his near hand now pointing above uke's head, or heavenward. The subtlety here is in the change of the attacker's grip, a change which can't readily be appreciated in the photo set: if done skillfully the attacker finds himself still trying to hold on with a clumsy grip, one on the verge of being outside the natural range of motion. This clumsy grip causes him to lean backwards trying to hold it, slowly breaking his balance. The lower dotted line shows us where tori's near leg will need to travel, and the upper where the balance breaker will begin.

Fig 3.2

Fig 3.3 sees the complete breaking of uke's balance as tori simply takes one more step forward. Tori does not need to sweep out his attacker's leg, aggressively push his attacker back or strike him but simply make a small shift forward with his own center of gravity. This causes uke's balance to break to the rearward due to an insistence to maintain a grip that is now weak and working against him.

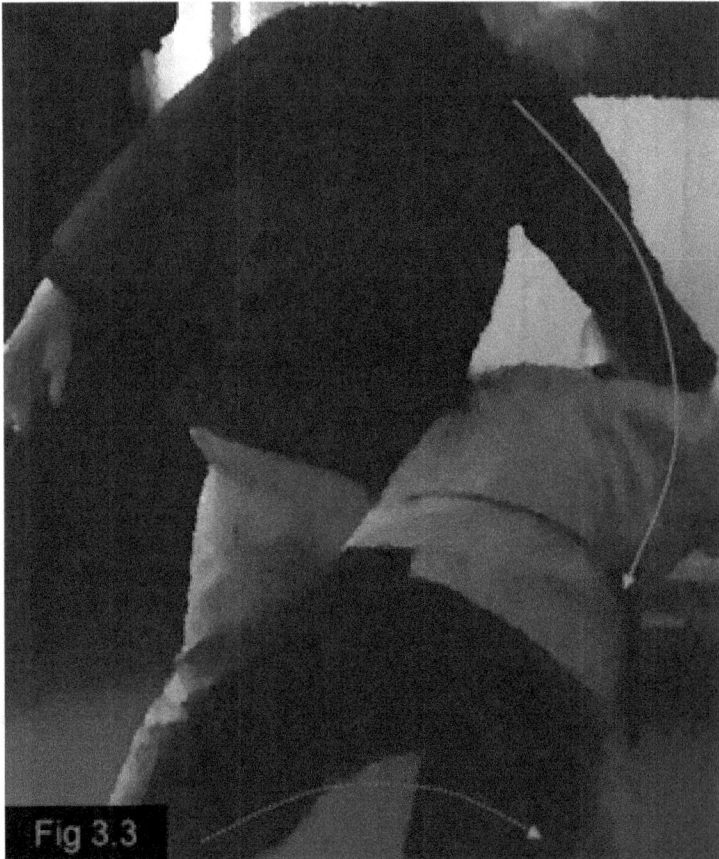

Fig 3.3

In the same attack, two wrists being held by two hands, a typical and classical Jūjutsu approach is as follows.

Fig 4.0 sees the clasp being made and held fast.

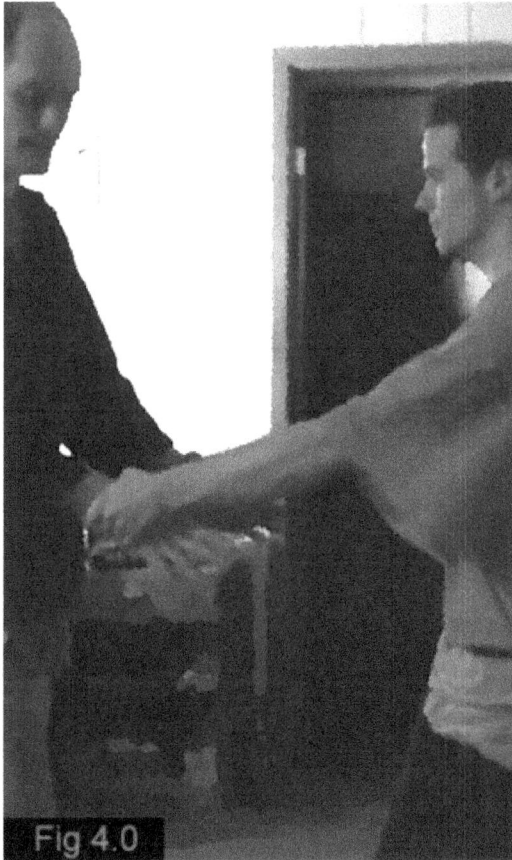

Fig 4.0

D. S. Hopkins

Fig 4.1 demonstrates a deft alteration to the attacker's grip by the defender, accomplished by moving his own hands: in this case he's twisted them palms up to the sky and away from the body, not unlike that seen in the Aiki-Jūjutsu maneuver. The straight upward arrows represent the upward movement of the forearms, while the curving arrows represent the turning motion of tori's hands so that they're palms-up.

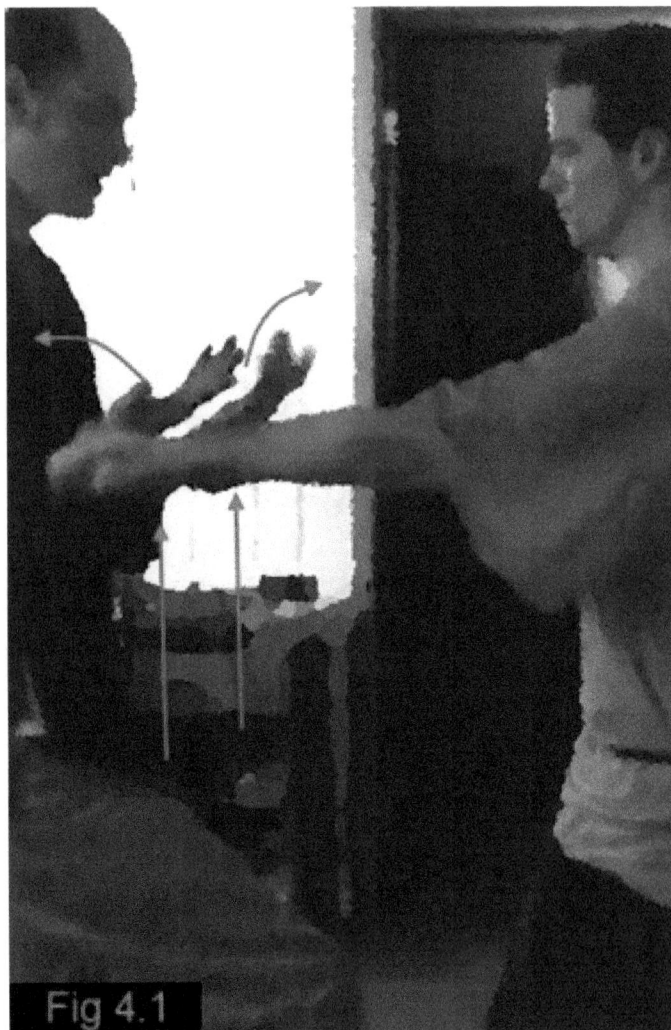

Fig 4.1

Fig 4.2 draws the eye to the outward position of tori's hands as uke's thumbs try to resist the outward movement and fail to hold them. Performing a restraining hold like this makes use of the finger's gripping strength, but routinely leaves the thumb exposed through isolation. The outward movements of the defender's arms here are working against the thumbs alone, and they are not sufficient to halt the movement, much less thwart the escape.

Fig 4.2

Fig 4.3 The new positions of tori's hands have followed a fast two step advance forward; one step to the outside of the attacker, and the other to a place just behind him. Tori's wrists are not only free, but now with the right hand horizontally situated across the attacker's chest and the left having returned the grip on the attacker by cupping his triceps (back of the upper arm) to control it, the positioning is set for a reap. The arrows to the top and bottom show the proposed forces, the bottom drawing back towards tori while the top one repulses; the curved arrow is where the right hand has traveled from.

Fig 4.3

Fig 4.4 is the complementary forces, low and high, being simultaneously executed to produce the leg reap and subsequently the balance breaking.

Fig 4.4

D. S. Hopkins

Fig 4.5 The final position of the maneuver has tori just above the attacker, still with a grip on the triceps of the right arm and with numerous opportunities for follow-up. The salient feature is not this position, because it is highly comparable to the Aiki-Jūjutsu maneuver prior to it, rather on the focus on the dual forces; the push and pull of the reap and the aggressiveness of the principles being used. In these particular examples the escape mechanics are actually common between the two systems, and a study of each will reveal that both use similar leg reaps and hip tosses and arm locks and so on. The difference is not in what one does that the other doesn't, but in where they choose to place emphasis. That emphasis decides ultimately how the system is used and can be used. Jūjutsu techniques are always direct, and perhaps more definitive than Aiki-Jūjutsu techniques, whereas the latter are almost always indirect, and perhaps more deceptive. Jūjutsu focuses on refinement of usage, her sister on refinement of principle.

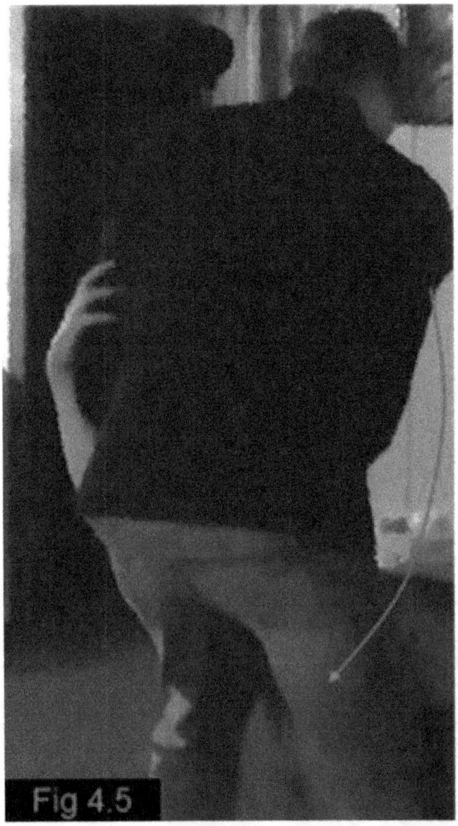

Fig 4.5

What Is *Jiu Jitsu*?

Jūjutsu uses a great deal of joint-manipulation itself, but for as much use as it makes of every kind of joint, tendon and musculature attack, it doesn't explore the intricacies of balance and position the way its sister does.

Jūjutsu places more reliance in weight-shifting, leveraging the mechanics of lift and principles of balance to use the entire body to affect throws, sweeps and balance breakers. This is knowledge dearly beloved of wrestlers and *judoka* and students of *Sambo*. And like the focus with which Aiki-Jūjutsu uses skeletal locks to meet its operational goals more than in Jūjutsu, here the proportions are reversed. What Jūjutsu does so well and often, Aiki-Jūjutsu only utilizes lightly, if at all.

Where they differ the most in practice is in the realm of the horizontal situation: Aiki-Jūjutsu goes to the ground little, while Jūjutsu has an array of maneuvers set aside specifically for this eventuality. Even their break falls, *Ukemi*, are mirrors of one another. But this is where the mirroring ceases as the Jūjutsu student continues after the fall to pursue an understanding of how to move and not to move when laying down to grapple with a foe.

When considering the willingness and proficiency of Jūjutsu to engage the enemy on the ground or floor, it's a good idea to be reminded of Judo, and how these judoka – students and teachers of Judo – use their anatomies to affect the balance breaking principles that topple one another or allow them to dominate the other on the mat. Jigoro Kano, the founder of Judo, removed what he felt were the most brutal and lethal parts of Jūjutsu to create a combat discipline that could eventually become a combat sport. In this enterprise he succeeded, and Judo became a combat sport that enjoys worldwide popularity today.

Its striking maneuvers removed, its rolls and throws and sweeps and pins emphasized, Judo yet remains Jūjutsu's offspring, despite much of its lethality having been subtracted. As such it still clearly demonstrates those principles that made its parent system so formidable in positions of tight and close grappling: the techniques of lift to apply take-downs to the target; the weight-shifting to break the target's balance; the leveraging of the stronger parts of the anatomy against the weaker for locks and chokes; and the repositioning of anatomy during entanglement to prevent the other's escape or improvement of position, while protecting those things for one's self.

The founders of Brazilian Jiu Jitsu built and improved upon this, the newest of Jūjutsu breeds, and this is especially true of those latter skills that include subtle repositioning of anatomy and the leverage not only needed to produce locks and chokes, but to move the entirety of the other person's body to better the position of one's own. In recent years the system of fight exported from Brazil has proven so uniquely specialized, tight and controlled when maneuvering on the ground, reminiscent of those traits so often exhibited in Judo and inherited from Jūjutsu, that it has gained global popularity in what seems like just a few short moments. The deep committal to one particular sphere of fight, namely ground mechanics, has provided it a mastery and dominance that few other martial arts can directly contend with. Exhaustive in conception and relentless in application, not many other disciplines display a level of refinement capable of direct contestation. Those that can - in many ways the peers of Jūjutsu, experts in the same school of thought and same aspect of the fight environment - are Russian Sambo, Judo, Shoot Fighting and various forms of grappling that grew out of European traditions, especially those that are Grecian in origin. It is also of note that the Brazilian style of Jūjutsu isn't a singular offering from that nation, as it is also from there that *Luta Livre* (a variation of which is called *Vale Tudo*) was born as well and fielded with great success. This is essentially a discipline modeled in much the same way and is strikingly similar in scope of usage. It has a long history of rivalry with Jiu Jitsu in Brazil.

One of the dividing lines is that Jūjutsu's emphasis is almost entirely on the physical condition. Its incorporation of mysticism is present but minor in comparison to that which can be clearly seen in Aiki-Jūjutsu, where a much greater emphasis is on the meta-physical, or meditative practices, commonly found in the Asian martial arts. The prospect of taking on an intimate involvement with the spiritual beliefs of cultures outside our own, or beliefs and outlooks that simply may not be compatible with our own, is a necessary concern when considering the practice of combat disciplines born and steeped in the ideologies of other nationalities. It exists to a lesser degree in Judo, being more of a combat sport that has grown farther away from its ancestral roots, but is much more integral to the study of Aikido, an internal martial art – internal meaning a practice that is as much spiritual as physical – and places an almost central focus on the development of Ki, or internal energy. This reach for spiritual unity within the practice of Japanese combat disciplines is not new. It is readily observable in the Zen Buddhism found amongst other cultures in Asia and in many of their martial arts. To the reader that strives for an entirely physical experience, a combat education and nothing more, it should be said that there are Jūjutsu schools, as well as Judo, that focus little or not at all on spirituality, and almost or entirely on physicality alone. Any instructor of any school should be able to answer this, and provide an insight as to what the exact practices and curriculum of his or her discipline is. To this writer's knowledge almost all Brazilian models of Jūjutsu are chiefly physical, aspiring only to reach a combat standard of excellence, and not a mystical one.

Inseparable from Jūjutsu and Aiki-Jūjutsu were the sword disciplines they were intended to support, because first and foremost the battlefield was the province of steel - the habitat of the sword and the kind of instant death it delivered there - while the hand-to-hand disciplines were a part of the Samurai's training to ensure he should not fail to lose the sword, or lose combat effectiveness even though he temporarily be without it. These modes of Jūjutsu not only provided the Samurai with a chance to reclaim a weapon in the heat of conflict should he be disarmed, but they also provided within themselves tactics to prevent the disarm and serve retaliations against any who would try.

Many Jūjutsu and Aiki-Jūjutsu schools, as well as Aikido, still teach swordsmanship within their curriculum, though this is far from as complete or beneficial as studying the sword disciplines Kenjutsu, Iaijutsu, Kendo or Iaido for themselves.

Already the reader can appreciate the genealogy of the martial art in question. Between Jūjutsu and her sister art Aiki-Jūjutsu, we have as offspring Judo, Aikido and all the modernized variations of the original two that have come down to us through the centuries.

Chapter 2

The Origins of Jūjutsu

The terms that comprise Jūjutsu are *Ju* and *Jutsu*, *Gentle* and *Art*, and the reaction people have to their translation is expected as they are immediately associated with their everyday usage in contemporary English, not even necessarily as they are defined. Linguistic misperceptions, widened by personal connotations, and then compounded further by a cultural gulf, make the reactions of people, though tiresome, naturally predictable when they first hear Jūjutsu translated. Like anyone else, an Occidental (a person whose ancestry is Caucasian) who hears a word like Jūjutsu translated for the first time, then and there places it within the context of their own society's usage. This results in a stalled comprehension of sorts, a kind of confused pause, as they try to reconcile their own understanding of the words gentle and art to a violent martial discipline of feudal Japan.

To understand Jūjutsu as the name of one of Japan's most violent martial arts, one must first understand what was intended by the culture that named it. Also, what is paramount to our consideration is the lack of genuine information (or the desire of the majority of people to even look for it) and of course the enduring presence of misinformation.

It's easy to see why an observer would come to any number of conclusions about the meaning of Jūjutsu in the absence of an understanding of Kanji, the Japanese writing system. If, for a few moments only, we ignore the literal meaning of what is meant by *soft skill* or *gentle art*, and imagine that people encountering the translation for the first time have only these English terms to draw on, we can begin to appreciate the lack of clarity that presently exists, firstly among things as common as names and terms in foreign tongues, but also among any number of principles and concepts concerning martial arts in general.

If the only information provided to an onlooker was the English translation of Jūjutsu, and then coupled with that was an opportunity to actually observe the martial art in motion, the observer might well conclude that the name gentle art was tactical in origin. They might think *Ju*, or soft, was making reference to the nature of the martial art's techniques, specifically how they can be applied with varying force, capable of inducing lesser or greater degrees of discomfort in an attacker, able to be increased or decreased in a closely guided manner, making it possible to chastise or humiliate an offender without necessarily having to kill him - this would be especially relevant if disciplinary action was required and not a death sentence. In such an example the name, *gentle art*, wouldn't be referring to the martial art's characteristics of application, but rather to its varying capacities for infliction; with a little imagination we can see how the term *gentle art* could be misconstrued to reference not the injury that such applications would produce in an adversary, but rather the possible *degree* of injury that could be produced.

The above example would represent the first misinterpretation.

Without knowing how to interpret the characters that represent *Ju* and *Jutsu*, one may even assume that the name was the result of a philosophical rationale. From a comparative perspective the decision to use words like *gentle art* of *soft skill* becomes especially poignant when the discipline is placed in direct contrast with those companion arts with which it was accompanied to the battlefield – martial arts that almost always killed instantly.

Those companion disciplines with which Jūjutsu worked so closely on the battlefield, and of which it was not the foremost skill-set in importance but rather somewhat auxiliary in usage, were disciplines such as *Kyudo* or Kenjutsu, which are the art of bow and sword respectively. Those arts were of the first importance and cannot ever – not in any culture of the period – be considered gentle in any way. Battlefield disciplines of archery and swordsmanship are not intended to plainly maim and kill, but to do it well and efficiently. It is most difficult to cut into an opponent or pierce them with a feathered projectile without disastrous result to life and limb, hence forever alienating such arts from ever being associated with words such as *soft* or *gentle.* In comparison Jūjutsu could quite easily seem gentle.

This above interpretation is no more accurate than the one before it of course, and only stated here to demonstrate how fast the truth can get lost without any guidance or understanding concerning terms from another language, culture and writing system as alien to us as the words they spell. How much more problematic would it be trying to understand the martial science the language describes, filled with all its complex processes, mechanics and concepts?

The truth of the name though? Linguistically, in the narrowest and most accurate sense, the Japanese character of *Ju* is understood to represent the idea of being soft, pliable or yielding. This softness or pliability is in relation to the malleability (or flexibility) of anatomy itself, or more accurately how anatomy is so affected by flexing forces during the maneuvers – the maneuvers, being processes represented by the word *Jutsu* - which are the actual skills themselves. Pliable techniques, or techniques of flexibility, while not as close as *soft skill* or *gentle art* is a still a rough approximation of what the name Jūjutsu communicates to us.

The Battlefield

First and foremost Jūjutsu was a fallback measure, a safety net or last resort for a Samurai in the event he should be disarmed during the course of the conflict. Within its wide scope of maneuvers are methods for conducting oneself, weaponless, against an armed and determined opponent. With his reliance on a training that had become reflexive and so had prepared him for the harsh and unforgiving realities of the field, a Samurai well-schooled in Jūjutsu could conceivably prolong his own life against a soldier or a swordsman long enough to rearm himself.

Off the battlefield the ruthlessness of a typical medieval society still prevailed, even if the violence had taken on a character that was less lethal than the front-line, but at other times more insidious and covert. This atmosphere had subordinates requiring discipline of the *dojo* variety (the *dojo* is a Japanese training hall for martial art practice), rivals requiring humiliation and possibly even death, and all of which could be required at a time when the sword wasn't necessarily within the *obi* (the obi is a belt worn about one's clothing) or even within reach – but Jūjutsu was a system of violence that could achieve all of it without ever having to draw the sword. The joint lock or choke hold that was restraining a man a second ago could very well be lethal a second later, depending on the needs of the moment: this type of versatility made Jūjutsu as highly applicable and practical in the sphere of political intrigues as it did in the service of one's feudal lord on the field.

A most attractive advantage to the martial arts, not only Jūjutsu alone but the full array of unarmed combat sciences, isn't only the inestimable empowerment it confers to the adherent or student, but also its invisibility. For the multitude of uses a warrior may have had for a martial art, not least of which would have been the ability to carry it into the presence of sensitive company, persons of power who would have prohibited weapons of any kind, to preclude the possibility of attack or assassination. Here is an education that instructs the mind in how to utilize the body as a weapon of bewildering potential, transforming the warrior into the very weapon he has been disposed of. All this is done with ideal clandestinity.

Consistent with militaristic thinking in any age or culture of the world is exclusivity. This is another of Jūjutsu's historical truths: the *bugei*, or martial arts, were reserved for soldiery and aristocracy and none of the lower classes had access to it. In particular instances one's clan could forbid the communication of family martial traditions and exercise a rigid guardianship of the discipline, and this can be seen in the *Daito-ryu* tradition where they allowed only Samurai of a specific region to have access to it.[1]

What Is *Jiu Jitsu*?

The Imperial family once maintained in high secrecy a combat art indigenous to the Minamoto family.[2] While in the very broadest sense they could also restrict any transmission of knowledge (military-related or otherwise) with a nation-wide edict.[3]

The priority of protecting combat maneuvers, what were really technical achievements in the way they were practiced, was not a concept that would become outdated as the years, decades and centuries unfolded. During the *Edo* period (1618 A.D. - 1872 A.D.) the various *ryus* (schools) made sincere efforts to ensure the secrecy of their methods through a policy of non-disclosure to anyone outside the school. This is not so surprising given that with the proliferation of armed and unarmed schools of every species up and down the nation's coasts, it would only be too expected that different types of expertise would distinguish one from another, and that those proficiencies would be the foundation of their success.

The exclusiveness of the *bugei* (or martial arts) to the military elite came to its almost complete terminus – with the exception of Ninjutsu and perhaps a few of the more vigorously guarded Aiki-Jūjutsu traditions – during the seventeenth century, after Tokugawa Ieyasu had forcibly brought the nation's feudal forces under one banner and gave Japan a solidarity that is called the *Muromachi* Period (or age of unification), which in essence was a general peace two centuries long. It is during this time, this era of the country without war, that the Samurai's role underwent a shift from combatant in service to the feudal warlords to administrator for the now supreme Shogunate. This transition of era, from wartime to peacetime, had also another effect, one highly detrimental: those it hadn't ushered into the new sphere of management and bureaucracy, it left without any purpose or function whatsoever, demanding far less of these military elite to oversee the new establishment than the battlefields of the previous era had needed to create it. This left a very great number of Samurai to suffer at what must have seemed a cruel turn of fortune on some level, to suffer an unforeseeable fate of poverty and squalor as relics of a bygone age.

With so very many hungry, desperate, masterless and penniless *Ronin* (this was a term for unemployed Samurai and translates as 'Men of the Waves'), they turned to fighting for money, dueling, working as hired swords, and in some cases teaching their skills to the lower classes in an attempt to stave off starvation and destitution. This development not only affected many of the warrior aristocracy but also impacted another warrior elite – the Ninja. At this time many of them had turned to banditry and robbery in an effort to feed themselves and survive the miserable fate that had been inflicted on them. It was a truth that would cause Ninjutsu to be outlawed for roughly three centuries, forcing its clans to conceal their practice and hand down their teachings in what we could term a hermetic secrecy. It is something more than amazing that the discipline survived and has since been identified as a

45

cultural heritage – it was only made legal again in the 1970s. As for the Samurai who had become the teachers of the schools that then had sprung up across the country, having bypassed the outlaw's life and unable to fulfill a role in the new bureaucracy, they became instrumental in the life cycle of Jūjutsu. They helped ensure the survival of the disciplines they'd themselves practiced, mastered and taken onto the field. In the schools of combat science that populate the Japanese landscape during the Muromachi period it is difficult not to see something of a mirror of the *salles d'armes* (drill hall) found in post-renaissance Europe.

It's hard to determine whether or not this disclosure of elite combat practices to the public was a good thing. On one hand it certainly meant these arts would have a better chance of cultural survival in the long term as the more people studying it it was less likely that the particulars of its practice would become lost as they did in the West (entire systems of fence using everything from Arming Sword, to Long Sword, to Great Sword, to Side Sword, to Rapier to Court Sword were lost in the West, as well as robust systems of hand to hand combat, as effective and complete as modern Judo.[4] This represents a loss of incalculable damage to historians, anthropologists, archaeologists, hoplologists and Western culture as a whole). So while martial arts such as Jūjutsu would be spared from the ignoble fate of being lost in a distant and disregarded past, the fate endured would be somewhat less glorious than its past life in the Age of the Country at War (also called the *Sengoku Jidai*, and was a period of constant warfare in medieval Japan) even if it did guarantee survival. That fate was dual-faceted: firstly, it involved proliferation of the military teachings in the hands of people outside of the retired Samurai once their lifetimes had expired; secondly, it involved battlefield disuse. This cannot be irrelevant. If necessity is the mother of invention, then disuse would have to be the mother of degradation. The battlefield's existence and continuous demand for qualified means meant that a constant standard was in place, an unbiased form of metric to assess the worth of all brought onto it. Once the battlefield was removed so too was the reliable discrimination it so consistently provided and that constant standard providing a safeguard to quality lost. Therefore degradation – with very small exception - would become the new constant.

Chapter 3

Degradation And Restoration

An unconventional point of view, encountered at whiles in other literary works, is the notion that these combat disciplines were improved in the absence of warfare. This is not supportable. Certainly improvements occur at different times and for different reasons in all fields of practice, but the suggestion that a general and ongoing improvement occurred in the absence of any tactical implementation is not considerate of an elementary truth: without a practical purpose a thing very rarely survives, let alone grows and thrives. How this peculiar persuasion came to acceptance, even to a minor degree, is an oddity, particularly since the only accurate means of assessing a martial art's effectiveness would require a testing method that would ensure the discipline could operate under the most severe conditions without any supporting factors to assist it. The results would need to reflect the performance of the martial art alone, ensuring the isolation of all other factors which might have benefited it, as much as humanly possible. The danger of failing to do this is obvious: if a martial art is measured for effectiveness in an environment that did not simulate the dangers exactly as they are in a worst-case scenario, then the perception of the discipline's effectiveness would not be in alignment with the realities it would be subjected to.

This means that the proposed assessment then would have to be carried out by a method wherein the results produced would be doubtless, enough that the examiner could be confident of entrusting his life to the martial art in question. The mechanism used for testing would need to be as free of imposed controls as possible: the harder and more unpredictable the conditions that the martial art would have to function under, the keener its effectiveness would have to be. This is likewise true for the opposite: the softer and more predictable the conditions that the martial art is practiced with, the less capable its effectiveness. The only true sphere for a successful trial is an uncontrolled environment, preferably under the most demanding and harshest conditions attainable – and that would be impossible without field applications in warfare.

Without an atmosphere of conflict by which to motivate change or prove the quality of those changes once they had been made, meaningful strides in development would have been narrowly limited. Modifications would not, of course, be impossible in a stagnant martial climate, just far less likely and far less beneficial. It is with the types of changes that we must be concerned, with their identity and then their value.

It is uncomfortably hard to term the changes that came to many of these martial arts during the Edo period peace as 'advances,' given that what they advanced towards was not in alignment with the needs of war for which they'd been created. To use the term *advance* then to describe these changes, without any further contextual clarity, would be to willfully mislead a reader to believe that the martial arts experienced a general betterment. This is not so. With proficiency in military operations no longer a priority, the changes these martial arts experienced was really not an advancement, but rather a *development* toward something new. Diminished but still functional, the role of the martial arts would now be one that would see them used on the roadways and pathways of Old Japan, serving the civilian and the ruffian.

Though this degradation was chiefly technical, the loss of quality wasn't limited to technicality. *Bushido*, the Samurai warrior code of conduct was – for the moment anyway - still an intrinsic part of the *bugei* or martial arts, but a moral degradation in the practice of those arts couldn't be avoided with the decline of the knightly caste to whom such disciplines had virtually belonged.

This becomes apparent in light of the wide and almost completely unrestricted availability of the martial arts to all those who existed outside the military aristocracy, where not only the honest, the law-honoring and respectable could make use of such knowledge to acquire expertise, but also the dishonest, the law-breaking and disreputable who'd be able to put it to every malicious use that the imagination could suggest. The long peace throughout the Edo period implies a pervasive tranquility that wasn't entirely true. This was due in no small way to that criminal element that no society has ever been without, but in this case they were disastrously empowered by a knowledge they hadn't had access to before and they were as well schooled in violence at that time in Japan as those whose responsibility it was to subdue them.[5]

This gradual demilitarization of the many combat disciplines would eventually translate into an impact on the curriculum, but this would not result in a high degree of change all at once, given that the chief change to be taken into account was in the political landscape, and it would eventually be that political change that would result in the changing of the martial atmosphere. Any significant differences would have been far ahead, much later in the Edo period than earlier. Part of this is probably due to the truth that for the first thirty to fifty years of the peace, most of the original Samurai who'd fought at the Battle of *Sekigahara* would still have been alive, and other Samurai in general, and as such some of the skill and experience from that era would've been still existent and vital - meaning the more pronounced changes in the martial arts would have transpired after a couple of generations had passed and these men had passed on themselves.

Throughout this long peace, roughly two and a half centuries, the curriculum of these martial art schools would lean ever more away from their militarized roots and ever more towards a demilitarized model, something much closer to civilian in nature. A Samurai or *Ashigaru* (foot soldier) or other member of the soldiery from the previous *Sengoku-Jidai* period would have trained in preparation for every danger, but would have had to borne constantly in mind the 'armed and armored' nature of the fight they were being prepared for. The 'armed and armored' reality, of course, belonged to the era that had passed, not the one unfolding. It's hard to imagine a member of the lower class studying an unarmed martial art in the Edo period with anything resembling the focus the combatants from the previous era would have had. The priority of these martial arts would eventually become the engagement of single opponents - under infinitely less turbulent conditions than a battlefield – eventually specializing in unarmed techniques against unarmored opponents.

In that myriad of *dojos* that dotted the Honshu landscape it's doubtful the unarmed schools continued any practice of *Yoroi-Gumi*, or grappling against armor, as time went on in the Age of Unification (the Muromachi or Edo period). Most of the studentry were not part of the soldiery but of the citizenry, and it was a time when the need for soldiery was in sharp decline, meaning there wouldn't have been a great motivation to learn the methods of grappling against armor.

During this Muromachi period the focus of grappling arts against unarmored opponents like Jūjutsu might be seen as a modernization, a step forward, especially given that by the end of the era armor would be on the decline. Most nations the Japanese encountered (particularly out of the West) had already moved past the medieval thinking that still prevailed in Japan, and their soldiers were unarmored. An occurrence of this sort though is more the result of happenstance than a calculated advancement: that a feature of the new training trend should pay off a century down the road wasn't a foreseeable event, rather a lucky one.

Probably one of the greatest developments to impact the martial sciences of Japan during the era in question was the refinement of those principles which combat techniques are built on. Principles that had been used for a long time, such as those at work when torquing an arm to execute a lock, that which uses one's weight to complete a throw, or the focusing of force to break an object with a strike, all found greater refinement of expression during that time.

This, however, was – and is – a two-edged sword. The principles were certainly refined, brilliantly in many cases, but not the techniques that used them. Herein lay the subtle self-sabotage: some of the techniques in the more traditional systems of Jūjutsu, when viewed objectively from outside the curriculum and with a discerning eye, seem to be made more to demonstrate the power of the principles they utilize than the process of effective application. This emphasis on the principles of the technique, as opposed to the technique (or process) itself, immediately alters the goal of the practitioner to some degree. If the aim becomes to illuminate the power of a particular effect instead of how that effect can be applied to meet the operational objectives, then already a shift has occurred carrying the system's maneuvers more away from an orientation that is pragmatic in execution and more towards one that is optimistic in composition. Whether this dangerous divergence in focus happens only a little or a lot in a martial art will greatly determine that system's odds of successful engagement and ultimately whether the product is effective in nature, or merely demonstrative.

Training within the *dojo* (or training hall) would in itself be only a small benefit in determining the quality of the product as the training hall doesn't emulate the actual environment in which the discipline will be required to function. The *dojo* would be a sea of tranquility by comparison to the proposed operational climate, and even the most aggressive training partner is still only that. Any competition, even one unregulated and organized for the sole purpose of advancing technical prowess within a school or between two different schools, though providing immensely superior combat simulation as opposed to *dojo* practice, can yet still only be so useful – especially given that it is but person against person attempting to win, not army against army attempting to kill.

Also, given that contests have standards that are uniformly applied to the opposing sides, it would be difficult to determine the worthiness of a maneuver, say one designed to respond to an armed antagonist with an unarmed solution, if the test-bed were a tournament format: the fact that most contests require their contestants to be evenly situated and matched at the outset would seem to prevent one from bearing arms and the other not so.

Despite all this there would be benefits to mat practice in the *dojo*, to contests between combatants and schools, and advancements would stem from the practice of both. But this would still not compare to the insights lost from application in broad-scale combat and tactical engagements where it's not just the fates of a few persons at stake, but rather that of entire dynasties and nations.

Tournaments can in some cases provide an experience that far exceeds that of *dojo* practice, assuming that the imposition of regulations hasn't divorced it too far from the operational realities of actual combat (some degree of deviation is expected, but too much is not only useless, it's also detrimental to perception). In the end if a martial art cannot be proven in the field, then competition becomes the next best choice for the sake of refinement and development: for without some way of sifting the functional components from the dysfunctional, without some way to detect and so correct the inefficiencies under varying types of stress, the technical weaknesses of these disciplines would never be rectified...only passed on to the next generation of students.

This truth for many readers can be difficult to appreciate, especially in the absence of the experience necessary to perceive it, an insight that rightly requires knowledge of multiple disciplines. And for those who possess such experience there is usually such a wide disparity of quality across the multitude of schools in the world that the above-mentioned deficiencies are as guaranteed to exist in some schools as they are guaranteed to not exist in others.

A further complication is that the schools in which the deficiencies do exist will be to unpredictable degrees and varieties. Compounding this is that not all persons involved, directly or as observers, are of the same perceptiveness. They simply may not notice where their curriculum is strong and where it's not, or if they do it may be that they don't possess the analytical skills to break down the particular practice, much less test it to determine the cause of the shortcoming and the best course for rectification.

Also, and perhaps more to the heart of the problem, is that we often don't want to see the shortcomings, failings or oversights in the endeavors we've spent so long pursuing. Who would? Really? To admit such things, even in the privacy of our own thoughts, shakes our confidence in the discipline in which we've invested so much; in ourselves as experts in an art we're now forced to question; and our instructors or martial role models who never forewarned us of any such weaknesses in our art, because in all probability they themselves had either never taken notice of it or refused to acknowledge the presence of an incongruity here and there. So the potential damage here can also reach out to taint the student's opinion of his mentor, left to decide whether the latter is either without ethics for withholding the discipline's limitations, or without competence of perception for failing to recognize them.

Often though the quality loss does not affect the entire system, but a few maneuvers here and there, and often the instructor doesn't see it not only because he's not looking for it, but because the far greater part of these combat disciplines are for the most part functional like a working machine carrying a fraction of discordant gears.

There is a deep mark of respect and statement of humility in the actions of a person who will not modify what they have learned, even to improve it, believing that the qualifications to do such a thing belong to more elite practitioners than themselves. This comes from a realization that it is with an old and veritable tradition that they would be interfering, for good or for ill. From this perspective the reservations someone might have are more understandable,when it comes to alterations of any kind concerning the discipline they practice, even if such an inhibition to restore the art's operability is more detrimental than not.

For many readers the notion of embarking on a long pursuit of the knowledge needed to prove these truths, locked and sometimes buried beneath mountains of related but not relevant material, is simply not feasible nor desirable. It is due to this that as the writer I have made every attempt to provide a sufficient treatment of the subject matter in a concise way that does not detract from the necessary length required by blunt honesty.

Most martial arts, but specifically the Jūjutsu and Aiki-Jūjutsu systems, that have come down to us in the present can usually be presented in a written state as a comprehensive index of maneuvers. These maneuvers address a broad scope of combative possibilities and subtleties, usually including within the curriculum the attacks, counters to attacks and every other supplemental aid practically required, and of course the underlying theory of operation. It is not uncommon to find within these indexes, that nearly comprise the entire system of fight to which they belong, more than a few dysfunctional maneuvers whose purpose it is to counter a specific attack. In reality they aren't equal to the task to which they've been assigned, not when considered in the violent context of an urban attack and infinitely less a battlefield.

The reasons for these dysfunctions have already been stated above, but the dysfunctions themselves will vary from one another and be set apart due to the nature of their failings. These failings can be assigned general types. The one obvious commonality that spans the entire collection of these deficient maneuvers, regardless of their type of failing or the system to which they originally belonged, is obviously their inadmissibility to usage in combat.

Some such deficient maneuvers are made so by being oversized. An overlong series of counter-moves are simply the result of being over-thought and not realistic, some in excess of ten motions long. One example was actually fifteen moves or better.[6] This type of departure from workable methodology is referred to in chapter six as a poorly designed chain technique, and will be explored there. For the sake of the topic at hand though, it'll be enough to assert that the inclusion of a counter-move whose likelihood of success is nil is more of a liability than an asset. It would firstly have the drawback of a low success rate (due to its length), and this in turn will force the martial artist to alter their game plan, possibly taking more damage than what was originally necessary. Secondly, the time and energy invested in its development would cause a subtraction of resources from techniques and developments that would've been more beneficial. And thirdly, and immeasurably worse, is that in a moment of crisis the dysfunctional maneuver will be totally out of sync with the demands of the task to be accomplished, conceivably leading to something worse than defeat.

If one imagines a physical altercation, a fight, and then further imagines all the rapidly changing positions, attacks, clinches and turns of fortune (a slippery patch, a distraction, a concealed weapon), the more complex a counter-move is, the less its chances of complete execution. Compare this now to an actual feudal battlefield, with all the thunderous din and screaming of men, neighing of horses, and clash of arms coming from every direction and at every range, from a foot away to half a kilometer. Thought of in these terms a technique fifteen moves long simply does not seem to fit, let alone allow its patron to survive in such an environment. And if the alternative view is taken, that the maneuver was intentionally designed to fight not on a feudal field of battle amongst many, but in an alley against one, then by virtue of design it had to have been constructed to succeed in such a predicament, but standing directly contrary to this is its unwieldy length – an unwitting frailty imposed by its designer.

It must be stated here out of the sincerest desire for fairness and accuracy that the presence of such an unwieldy maneuver, as that described in the passage above, does not immediately typify or categorize the entire system to which it belongs – it may be but one oversight in the larger design, one errant thread in the tapestry. In any case it cannot be allowed to color the impression of the discipline as a whole, only motivate a deeper scrutiny of it.

This weakness of excessive design may not seem like a grave impediment to the usage or to the success of a discipline, and in truth it isn't common enough to be deeply troubling by itself, but when taken into account with more typical failings it begins to become part of something larger: a perceivable, if inadvertent, disassociation with workable tactical tools, or more bluntly, a mistaken divorce from things that work.

A pattern of ineffectiveness starts to take definable shape as we see maneuvers – taught in the most serious training halls with the strictest etiquette – that presuppose an adversary who has attacked us (and is under the effect of fear, anger, panic and subsequently adrenaline) will be easily guided or handled much like an uke on the mat: directed with easy movements, graceful force and an absolute expectation of success. Not all schools are plagued with this type of shortcoming, but they do exist, and it creates a false impression of the type of resistance likely to be encountered in actuality, allowing the student to feel the beginning of a proficiency that is largely supported by an artificial control over the training partner that is preeminently hollow. This truth all but sets up the student for failure as they are being prepared for a circumstance that won't represent the prevailing conditions. An inflated sense of control, quite unfortunately, may not be an isolated failing in a *ryu* (school), but possibly indicative of an ongoing *dojo*-wide training practice.

Another force that often works in tandem with this exaggerated sense of control (both of which are considered early and temporary training aids) is an exaggerated sense of power, particularly visible in the person being subjected to the maneuver, the training partner. The policy is for students to use light-contact strikes and nothing too much heavier, or even shadow-striking (which is to say that no physical contact is being made with the target). The training partner receiving the mock-strikes behaves as if contacted by a heavier hit, miming the damage that would have been incurred in an actual fight to assist the person performing the maneuver. If not duly and appropriately abandoned at the correct stage of development this kind of practice can create a dangerous mindset in the student. The expectation of a constant favorable outcome begins to unconsciously take root (and so hinders or outright removes improvisational skill development). Despite this the student still develops a reflex-reaction, just not the desired one. The reflex reaction becomes a reply of minimal force instead of one of full, or at least adequate, force. In cases where the practicing student is executing maneuvers at full force they will be deliberately aiming to miss their training partner, and so substituting one unhealthy reflex development for another. Now, instead of under-powering their striking instruments, they choose to sabotage their ability to target with them. One type of conditioning is no less destructive than the other – this can be rectified by using shock-padding and impact-resistive gear to develop the correct reflex reactions, both for power and for accuracy, by allowing the training partner to absorb the violence using safety aids. Without correcting this and continuing to rely on under-powered strikes that cause an exaggerated sense of effect, or full-powered strikes that come no where near enough to the target, all motivation is removed to strive for the development of adequacy. To use a martial schooling instrument like this incorrectly, one that creates reflex reactions, will produce the completely opposite and undesirable result to what is actually intended: it stunts the studentry, leaving their reflexes for power-generation and targeting at an early stage of development. The muscle-memory conditioning which is traditionally, and so successfully, employed to create powerful martial artists, sabotages the aspiring pupils with effective programming that should have developed them through the endless thousands of repetitions...not undermined them.

Within schools where this is detected, it may not necessarily indicate a failing or deficiency: many schools use this type of training policy amongst students of earlier ranks to provide a real and useful study aid in developing those skill sets which are necessary. That said, it should not be a policy for every student at every rank, only an aid for students to achieve the competency needed to arrive at those later ranks. Equally invaluable is the policy to drop such training aids at the right stage of development so that the student of combat can progress. The concern here is those establishments that turn the modified schooling so typical in the early curriculum into a policy of training for the entire training hall for all students and at all ranks.

Comparable policies are sometimes witnessed concerning mass attack training, which is the schooling that prepares the student for multiple assailants converging on him from multiple directions. The end goal of training for a mass attack scenario is to build the skill sets necessary to intercept and manage more than one hostile arriving within tactical range at the same time. An anticipated failing is to instruct the student how to manage attackers in series, which is to say one after the other, and never arrive at a stage of progression where more than one is arriving at once. At the outset of such training it is naturally imperative to begin managing the assailants in series, first one, then the next, then another and so on to build the rapid reaction skills necessary to proceed. Without any progression beyond that stage – beyond the rapid defense in series – there can't be any complete preparedness, even though a very useful skill has been developed in dealing with high volumes of assailants in rapid succession, because allowing the student to believe that they can now be effectively surrounded and converged upon from multiple sides would be a betrayal of their trust.

Again, the reader must use discretion and discernment if ever investigating these truths from a first person point of view, taking greatest care not to unfairly or accidentally impugn or malign a school based on something incorrectly perceived or interpreted. These practices – if they do indeed pervade the entirety of the ranking system, top to bottom – are just not acceptable when careful consideration of the techniques in question are placed in even an approximation of the proposed environment where they'll have to either perform or, through an inability to perform resulting from catastrophic design flaws, destroy the student trying to apply them.

The notion that it would have appeared this way, been practiced this way, and handed down this way at a time when its sole reason for existence was to survive the rigors of warfare is unconvincing. Preparing a student, a soldier – a young Samurai! - for something less than the truth wouldn't only have been useless, it would have been dangerous, counterproductive and hence contrary to military goals. Outside of martial art disciplines – Eastern or Western – that have undergone heavy premeditated modernization for deployment in say police services, military or other field use, the only real historical exceptions to this degradation would be something like a concealed or otherwise protected tradition, experiencing little or no change, that still closely resembles its feudal roots.

Jūjutsu, like other disciplines in the same family and from the same region of the world, found itself still utilized during the peace and this would have preserved certain forms in something recalling the prime condition of the era before. But that truth could not vanquish another truth that without the demands of the battlefield, without the necessity for that tactical efficacy which warfare so unarguably dictates, the new impetus for practice would be something less than the requirements of combat. A new and less excellent tradition had then begun a slow development in other places (for the deterioration would have been languid), carrying the same name but possessing a technical quality becoming more coarse and unrefined. In theory multiple tiers of quality would have been coming into coexistence unlike anything before: the first standard, that which prevailed amongst the teachers (the schooled and accomplished military gentlemen - the Samurai - who belonged to and were forged in a more turbulent time of the generation before); and the second standard would have been the greater majority of persons pursuing the skills in an era where war was more of an anomaly and peace more of a constant.

The longer these conditions persisted the worse the degradation would become. It would be unavoidable, despite any one school's or master's most earnest attempts to prevent it through maintaining their own high standards as the breadth of practice on a cultural level by person's operating with little or no oversight would defeat any uniformity in quality. Variances in martial quality would have been present in the Sengoku-Jidai as well, that era of warfare predating the long peace – this goes without saying – but the assertion here is that it would have been significantly worse in the time ahead, following the great expansion of practice across the country. One needs only to regard any modern school today of a particular specialty and then compare it with other schools of the same study: a minimum degree of expertise across all the schools is nearly guaranteed, but so is a disparity in standards, government oversight notwithstanding. It would only be with the strictest quality control, on an executive level of leadership, like that found in the Armed Forces that there would be anything like conformity to a single standard. In any other field of study, inequality amongst schools, a little or a lot, is all but assured. It's difficult to imagine the plight facing the history of Jūjutsu being much different.

Yet though these disciplines were diminished by disuse, they certainly didn't perish and their quality was sufficient to hold up across almost forty decades and survive to today. That, however, doesn't dismiss the problems, but it does prove that these martial arts could survive despite them. The truth of this longevity cannot be reduced to any one factor, but perhaps two: the first is that despite the many deficiencies and inefficiencies that eventually came to plague these disciplines, not all these cancers were allowed to flourish, because there were and would always be those perceptive, thoughtful and creative personalities seeking to cure and enhance whatever system of fight they used. And though on the whole the corrections would be lopsidedly outnumbered by the deviations, they'd still have a not inconsiderable enriching effect that would help stem the decay. The second factor is plainer: the remarkable effectiveness of Jūjutsu today, and Aiki-

Jūjutsu as well, are evidence of descent from an immensely powerful feudal root, that though reduced by neglect, still retains a potency able to overcome the greater part of challenges presented to it.

In light of all that has been said regarding this greater vitality of the martial arts in the feudal era as opposed to what came later, even compared to what we have here today, there exists a view that martial arts needn't be capable of actual combat to be worth practicing and there is a cultural, moral or historical benefit to be gained from their study, even if there isn't anything immediately practical. This is an odd line of reasoning if one stops and considers that the primary function of a thing – of anything – is the very reason for its existence and everything else is a byproduct of that purpose. Stranger still is to chase these incidental gains as opposed to the essential one, the central one: in this case, combat proficiency. This rings especially true when you take into account that these other benefits can be had in many other places, and better so. Most people who make that most serious of investments in the pursuit of a thing – namely that of 'time' – usually aren't looking for something in general, but rather something in particular. And though the reasons for choosing to study a martial art can and do vary, one factor that is a constant regardless of reason is that the participants expect the curriculum to have some application value. Most disciplines do and so this usually isn't an issue, but the idea that a discipline can be dysfunctional and still valuable isn't reasonable. No amount of historical perspective (which many of these disciplines can't provide as they are too far removed from their medieval roots), or of that etiquette found in a Japanese tea ceremony or Buddhist doctrine, is going to attract and retain students to an Asian culture combat discipline that is no longer fit for combat.

This chapter has tried to illuminate the loss of direction that the martial arts experienced in Japan's 1600s and how that translated into a loss of quality over a span of time; and then the finding of a new direction that provided a new emphasis on the recreational more than the operational. From the Age of the Country at War to the Age of Unification, to the very moment that we ourselves now occupy, the Japanese martial arts have traveled so very far and undergone whole eras of change, with this last one perhaps yielding up a small ray of promise: with the popularity across the world for these disciplines on the rise, and the new expression given to these martial arts in MMA and other tournaments around the globe, an era of refinement has been underway since the early 90s in North America, and in other continents even earlier. The grittier tournament formats are being used to explore a martial art's combative viability and to sift out those components that have proved less than useful. Unfortunately there is a great many things that a tournament cannot qualify in a martial art, and without the battlefields that came before we find ourselves using whatever tools we have to verify or discard the tactical efficacy of a discipline's maneuvers. The struggle is for reliable testbeds of effectiveness; and tournaments – limited though they be – are still somewhat useful in that regard.

War And Games

Throughout history war precedes the subsequent war games. Competitions concerning the combat sciences, regardless of where they originated, who made them or of what kind of contest they'd been, armed or unarmed, horsed or unhorsed, were still all exactly that, a type of war game. Empty hand is no doubt the most senior, the oldest records reaching back to ancient Greece. The Romans built and filled their great arenas with a plethora of gladiatorial scenarios. Perhaps the best example of war games that emulated battlefield conditions were the jousting tournaments that pervaded medieval Europe – bloody and violent affairs that required martial skills begun no later than childhood. But what of combat sciences that survived in a recreational capacity long after they had become anachronistic and fallen out of usage? Combat practices that eventually forgot their own lineage and became something entirely new?

In the West professional boxing, Olympic wrestling and sport fencing would each find themselves in this category, having started as something combative, necessary and dangerous in a time long before. In the East Judo is an excellent example of such a combat sport, as is Taekwondo and Karate. In recent years the Brazilians, chiefly the *Gracies*, managed to export their nation's own tournament formats to the rest of the world, resulting in the rise of the MMA and competitions that promote it. The effect of converting combat practices into competitive forms is what must become the fixation of our attention here. What effects does the creation of an environment, standardized and regulated, controlled and promoted, for the purpose of professionalized competition have on the combat traditions that participate?

We must make this inquiry, and most earnestly, to understand the very real and vast divides separating combat sports and combat disciplines – because they're two entirely unique offspring from a common parentage. As much as a martial art has in common with its combat sport sibling, there is equally as much that is distinctive and sets them apart. Once a martial art becomes a structured sport that encourages non-lethal rivalry a degree of change ensues. While the considerably different conditions of a new operational environment demand this modification, it creates a predictable and debatable mix of enhancements, additions and amputations that essentially sees the birth of something altered enough to be classified as *new*.

The first enhancement in the installation of a competition model of a martial art is promotion of that art, simply meaning that it usually translates into exposure to a wider audience that in many cases never knew the combat art in question existed at all. The nature of competition is as much a recreational activity for the audience that watches as it is a professional activity for those who fight within it. That means instant marketability, instant exposure to a wider viewership and hence a greater awareness on the part of people in general concerning it. Many such martial arts enjoyed this type of popularization in the early part of the 1990s as MMA made its debut in parallel with Gracie Jiu Jitsu.

When a martial art becomes more visible to the masses it normally follows that there is a greater interest and subsequently a greater enrollment in the study of that art. From a short term perspective this increases the discipline's popularity, in the long term its lifespan. It may initially sound absurd to contemplate a martial tradition's lifespan with so many people on the globe, and so many practicing...but consider it: not a French Musketeer, a British Dragoon, a Spartan Hoplite, a Roman Centurion or a Knight of the Order of the Temple of Solomon would have believed that the sword they carried, lived by and conquered with would not only disappear, but wouldn't leave barely more than a glimmer to anyone who came afterward as to how to use such a weapon. And each of those examples belonged to some of history's most formidable warrior traditions. Lifespan matters – and the longevity of any combat practice has to improve in direct correlation with the number of people that propagate that practice.

One of the inevitable impacts to a martial art achieving rapid popularity is the nearly instant demand for more qualified persons to supply that discipline. If the demand for instructors can't be readily met it isn't difficult to determine that quality control could fast become a casualty, and with more and more students being taught, the levels of instructor investment are either disproportionate or just generally lower across the group as a whole. This quite easily becomes the reality if the instructor-to-student ratio ends up redistributed to favor high student capacity as opposed to high student development.

This tends to happen when whatever is being taught comes into wide demand: instructors find themselves attempting to manage much larger student loads than what their experience has prepared them for. Compounding this overload dilemma is the martial art community itself, as it doesn't exactly use stunningly efficient business models: schools are usually limited to one *dojo*, and only in real rare cases has an instructor branched out to become a small chain of schools. However, far more often than not it's the former – schools are small, single training halls with a very limited production capability.

The motivation to teach due to passion as opposed to profit is, of course, quite natural. Also is the reality that their own instructors probably taught for the same reasons. A *dojo* being operated like a non-profit school and not like a for-profit business isn't going to require tailored marketing strategies, an efficient and effective organizational hierarchy, informed resource allocation or time investiture on behalf of the owner/operator. These considerations will be plainly nonexistent. A *dojo* that exists to further the study of a martial art doesn't exist to generate revenue, and being such doesn't require those business structures or processes to accomplish financial success. For a student schooled in such a *dojo*, their instructor has unconsciously taught them to teach the very way he himself does. They've been instructed – indirectly perhaps, but instructed nonetheless – to forward a martial art, not facilitate a financial enterprise. It's important to realize the difference, because from an administrative perspective they are not the same thing.

And considered from this perspective we can safely assume that most instructors – being of a serious disposition concerning the academic integrity of their discipline or sport – make an earnest effort to strive for quality of students, not quantity of students. Most schools then are small in floor space, small in student attendance, but have a higher degree of instruction per student, producing martial artists of greater quality than what might be typically found in a larger facility (unless that larger facility has a staff of instructors). Loss of quality is caused by nothing more extraordinary than a sudden shift in media exposure that causes an influx of new recruits and thins out instructional resources. Despite this damage to quality from overloading, there are other quality-losses from other quadrants that are every bit as severe.

Not all instructors are equally skilled in their disciplines, in their talent to instruct or in their leadership of a group. This truth is important to note and understand: not all skills related to instruction and management of the training hall are necessarily a part of the martial education itself. Not all instructors are capable of producing instructors, and some can barely produce proficient students, even when they themselves are outstanding martial artists. Outside of the martial curriculum are other skills that are simply for the most part not considered, not taught and most of the time not even present. The simple observation that teachers come in different ranks – from *Sensei* to *Shihan* to *O Shihan* – does not illuminate the possible shortcomings of people in supervisory positions. There exists many great martial artists, phenomenal even, that do not possess the necessary skill sets to adequately instruct someone else in the practice of what they can do so very naturally. Communication skill from the outset will decide much of an instructor's effectiveness – can he merely speak the language he's teaching in? Or can he *wield* it? Can he control a loud and obnoxious room that is adversely energetic? Or is he controlled by it?

Not many martial arts schools impose quality controls on instructor-ship or have a viable instructor training program, rather they learn the essential basics from their *Shihan* or master and teach as they've been taught. This creates a cycle of emulation; the student adopts his instructor's teaching methods and never changes them for good or for ill. Once in a long while a school, or small chain of them, will emerge with a mentor-program and a little more sophisticated approach to mass instruction – but it's usually only the very best business models that can do that.

And yet for all that these schools could gain with instructor-training programs and the increased quality of both the teachers and students they produce, the martial arts are significantly damaged by things much more insidious. If a student new to golf tries to teach himself how to swing a driver he runs a high risk of injury. If, however, he entrusts his education to a professional instructor, only to find out through a severe shoulder strain that the teacher was not a practitioner but only a pretender of the sport, then the student is even worse off than he would've been in a self-taught scenario. At least someone self-taught will go out of their way to discover, first and foremost, how *not* to do it. There are no such guarantees that the pretend-instructor will do even that much.

This analogy becomes yet more sobering when we make a direct comparison of these athletic ventures, and specifically the study of each. The study itself must be our focus, not the difficulty of studying one or the other. How much inherent risk is there in trying to learn a combat discipline under the tutelage of someone who is inept and unqualified? Far more than what there is in golf, certainly. And golf would be dangerous enough if an idiot was teaching it – never mind something violent in nature. It exists as one of the most dangerous threats to the quality of these disciplines and sports, and arguably the most to the safety of the people practicing them: the pestilence of pretenders. As the popularity of a martial art reaches some critical plateau it attracts attention not only from potential students, but from exploiters. These operational difficulties and professional frustrations are a lamentable reality for all those qualified and credible schools out there, trying to run despite them. The respectability (quite aside from prestige and appeal) of any discipline suffers from the humiliation of being represented by the incompetent; this then further becomes compounded by the detraction of spectators who are unable to detect the counterfeit.

As preposterous and unlikely as this account that follows below may seem, the reader is reminded that it isn't nearly so improbable as a first thought might suggest. While fictional, the narrative below has been pieced together from multiple sources and washed, dyed and retold to preserve anonymity, but the most pertinent elements are preserved for their accuracy.

The Encounter With Ole' Triple J

The word was that around the corner near old downtown, "Jiu Jitsu Jerry" or good Ole' Triple-J as his past students called him, was teaching out of his newly opened MMA gym. Proudly hung in the window was a Brazilian flag along with a Canadian and possibly a Japanese one – the last two looked more like curtains though, not hanging right side up and more than a little raggedy. There was a Portuguese slogan written across the Brazilian one, whereas the words on the other two were just graffiti. Through the glass Jerry could be seen, standing here, standing there: he looked cool, cool and in control, not ever concerned about anything. He laughed and reclined back in a chair near the wall. It was a mint-condition foldout lawn chair. He laughed again. Every so often his expression and body language sobered up and he could be seen through the glass saying something to somebody, but most of the time he was content just to watch from his chair, often looking down toward the floor. There were little kids on the mats, half a dozen or more. To a passerby, someone casually interested, they seemed to be trying to do moves that were somewhat half-familiar, something reminiscent of...something; or maybe it was nothing more than just the hapless tumbling of little kids in karate uniforms. The paper flyers, and there were more than a few, hanging on the inside of the glass door said that Jerry was an expert at a bunch of different things: Brazilian Jiu Jitsu was only one of them.

It was best just to keep watching, do some window shopping before committing to a buy, no different than any passerby in any Turkish Bazaar: one mustn't engage the haggling merchant without knowing as much as they can about the product first. Eventually it became clear what he was staring down at. He was texting or playing a phone game. Suddenly he looked up at the kids and snapped some instruction at them, annoyed. The friend who recommended Jerry said he was an expert in a bunch of different martial arts. The flyers reveal the flattering claim that the hero in the lawn chair knows four disciplines. It's just a stray thought...but, but wouldn't that take a long time to learn? One. Two. Three. Four. Four different martial arts. Doesn't it take quite some time just to learn one? And Jerry looks no older than twenty-two. Somewhere during all this Jerry had gotten up and left his captain's chair. The time has come to step through the glass door, ask a few polite questions, and try to decide if this guy should be paid for anything.

Looking back now this must have seemed like the gateway to an alternate universe for Jerry, where fantasy became reality, but for the discriminating consumer – dust up the nose, the moldy smell, the shoddy insufficient lighting that forces the eyes to squint – it was more like one of those utility areas that janitors have access to in shopping centers, those places that the patrons never see. Jerry is nowhere around. The kids are wandering about. A few are looking out the window. More are sitting on the floor doing nothing.

A television was playing a room or two away. An early UFC rerun. Jerry was intent. Pausing, slowing, now replaying the video segment...then repeating the entire process...he was absolutely absorbed by this one section of video. He watched it, bug-eyed, over and over and over. An entire minute expired before he actually took note of the potential customer waiting in the hall.[7] As strange as it had appeared, it almost seemed that Jerry had been –

attempting? - to reenact what the fighters were doing on his own dusty floor under bad lighting. Jerry, expert in four disciplines that he was, could've been critiquing the twenty-three-year-old fight on the screen by reconstructing each fighter's mistakes...Perhaps he was comparing their archaic techniques to his own masterful moves? He was present and in the room now, the mime slapped out of him, no longer reliving the old video reenactment, and was trying to answer the question he'd just been asked about classes.

Classes. Right. He'd been asked about *classes*. First lessons consist of what? What are the names of the things that would be learned?

Jiu Jitsu Jerry said that the names aren't as important as the moves themselves.

What moves? What's going to be learned? He's asked again.

He stands facing the questioner, said it's better to learn defense first, so he starts with teaching Judo and then Aikido, then moves on to something more Chinese. *Judo annnnnd Aikido*. There's a combination that could easily tie up three quarters of a decade. Okay. It was just about time to get out of here. A look at Jerry reveals he's attempting to balance himself in some bizarre stance accompanied by a goofy dipping motion, and this can only prompt a second-last question: what bones, joints, musculature or aspect of a person is this posture, this *dip*-attack, of Jerry's supposed to be attacking?

The name of a bone isn't as nearly as important as knowing how to break it says good Ole' Triple-J.

Now it *was* time to go. He was walking behind, talking fast, pitching... pitching fast... trying a sales pitch to sell his 'advanced super fighter program.' The glass door was ahead with its absurd flyers; the front window was next to it, curtained with the Brazilian flag. The departure was put on hold. This truly was the very last question: what does that slogan mean, the one in Portuguese written across the middle of the flag? *Ordem E Progresso*?

Triple-J answered, too cool even for himself: "It's about martial arts. Jiu Jitsu". Disgusted. Departure resumed. It was actually the Brazilian National Motto, *Order and Progress*, because it can be seen in any number of places, and it's nothing to come across it while say shopping on Amazon.

Well, every reader ought to know that the modern world is absolutely teeming with Jiu Jitsu Jerrys and their breed. In point of fact they're almost more common than the actual instructors. The determined reader who has already decided to study Jūjutsu of any kind (or any martial art for that matter) is going to have to prepare themselves to undertake a diligent search. Some people have expressed a dislike for the style of etiquette typically found within Japanese *dojos*; the bows, and lower bows, and bows from the *seiza* (or sitting position), and the clapping and the formal addresses when speaking to the *Shihan*. This is entirely the prerogative, preference and right of the prospective student, but of all the positive things that can be said for the presence of etiquette, structure and culture and discipline for example, it does have one other benefit: it's one more piece of authentication the Jiu Jitsu Jerrys mess up on because this complex cultural formality allows us to detect them a little easier. In the end, however, the Jiu Jitsu Jerrys aren't limited to any one discipline in any one place. Whatever enjoys the greatest surge of current popularity is usually that which is mostly at risk from the pretender community. It happens all the time, martial arts becoming Triple-J magnets.

This has been and will always be an unfortunate truth and drawback of popularity: everyone wants to be the expert, and so few ever make it that far. And then, once in a while it seems, someone is found pretending to be the expert. Only it's not once in a while, it occurs with disastrous frequency. It's not only an insult and devaluation to those who genuinely succeeded in the acquisition of their expertise, it's dangerous to those who are deceived and submit to unqualified instruction not knowing any better, because these phonies aren't pretending to have credentials at tennis or badminton or soccer but an aggressive combat art.

This isn't to imply that the Brazilian Jiu Jitsu school you're considering needs to be personally taught by Kid Peligro, Rodrigo Gracie or Saulo Ribeiro, but certain constants aren't unreasonable to anticipate. While the techniques themselves don't definitely require their names to be in Portuguese, or Japanese if the Jūjutsu is in the Asian mode, it would be more natural if there were at least references made to maneuvers in the mother tongue from time to time. There should also be a logical technique progression, nothing chiseled into stone but an accurate guideline of some kind, and in concert with that a skill progression represented by rank. There should also preferably be something, some evidence, any at all, lending validity to the claims that are being made. In the case of our Jiu Jitsu Jerry above knowing four different styles of fight, unless they're closely related, it isn't that common (absurd by the age of twenty-two) – and there should be some sort of hard copy proof, other than the computer-generated flyer on the wall, next to the price list for *Jerry's Deluxe Double Value Champion Packages*.

Now, just because Jiu Jitsu Jerry didn't prove to be a responsible person to invest your money and time with, much less trust with your safety, that's not to say that the next guy you run into with a gym downtown doesn't know his business. He doesn't need to be fluent in Japanese or Portuguese either, nor have a degree in medicine focusing on skeletal anatomy, but the man's expertise should be apparent in the way he conducts the education of white belts compared to say blue belts and so on. The preposterous Jiu Jitsu Jerry cited up above hopefully communicates this reality to the reader, but the ugly truth is that the fictitious Jerry actually falls quite short of the real Jerry that was the basis for this story: it was nothing less than an egregious vacancy of qualifications. The absence of responsibility, the spaced-out disregard for the safety of others, and then the shamelessness to demand payment for it all could have only left those suckered by the farce feeling like they'd been unwittingly made a part of something sickly comedic. A tasteless prank.

Another benefit of martial arts that become the basis for competitive sports is that they tend to attract people who would not otherwise have ever invested time and energy in them. In some cases they've even become Olympic sports and reached that highest pinnacle of accomplishment that a sport can. This also has the not dismissible benefit of bringing people to athletics as a profession, especially in the case of Olympiads, to become career athletes and reap physiological rewards regardless of podiums and precious metals. The inclusion of such talented athletes into a combat sport's pool of participants provides not only a prestige to the sport practiced but also allows it to be expressed with a competence that may have not existed up until the performance of a particular person. Some of the most exciting and excellent combat sciences that have ever been were recognized not only for their innate virtues, but for the legendary prowess of some exceptional personage that utilized it, immortalizing not only themselves but the means they used as well.

Someone could conceive an immensely powerful combat art, but if they have no one willing to invest themselves in its development, then they in the end only have an intangible thing, a concept. The consequences of a tradition dying out due to lack of adherents isn't so different from the non-existence of one that couldn't attract any to begin with. To look back behind us, to Japan in the late *Heian* or early *Kamakura* period, round about the latter part of the twelfth century, it's strange to envision a nation where the *Iga* and *Koga* clans were not shaped by Ninjutsu. Those mountain clans represent the physical embodiment of the Ninjutsu tradition, which before them existed only as a range of complementary concepts, ideas and arts. For the *shinobi* to exist someone somewhere first had to invest themselves in the new philosophy. Without people willing to commit to the practice of a discipline, to uphold a tradition or begin a new one, implosion and finally discontinuation are the only result. Popularization through sportsmanship has the effect of countering this implosion.

Chapter 4

In The Field

The nature of a combat discipline is to war; to fight without restriction or reservation. Before they were sports, martial arts were products of necessity, only set aside when the need for which they were created was met by better means. Stated as such we can expect to lose a practice as soon as it's obsolete, as the weapons are replaced by better weapons. Yet hand-to-hand methods have the special distinction of having an instrumentation that is quite irreplaceable. The weapons of the unarmed disciplines are of course the human anatomy itself, and as such makes the hand-to-hand arts stand apart from weaponized disciplines that have a far more limited applicability in the modern world, or whose implements – be it the sword or the spear – have been relegated to total disuse and abandonment. Yet that same modern world sees a near total applicability of unarmed disciplines such as Jūjutsu in a breadth of occupations: soldiery, security, field operations, policing and executive protection. This ongoing need has provided an impetus for maintaining and utilizing hand-to-hand systems of fight the world over, and even a few of those weaponized disciplines (Karate's use of the *tonfa* for example).

While the benefits of competition-arts has already been stated, and they are numerous, their existence for many combat disciplines doesn't represent survival of the discipline it descended from (that in many cases having been lost long before) but rather the final deterioration to a state no longer capable of any tactical implementation. The benefits then of the competitive modes of a martial art have to be assessed for their negative impact as well as positive, especially when an art that a sport was based upon has morphed so completely as to leave no glimpse of the former in the presence of the latter.

The discontinuation of the combat discipline then becomes a loss to the culture that employed it, an injury even. The historian, the anthropologist, the archaeologist, to name but a few, can only truly gain any insight using such arts as a component of their research if those arts cast something of an accurate reflection of the time in which they originated. Whether it be the historian's pursuit of history, the anthropologist's pursuit of combat arts as they affected people or the archaeologist's pursuit of understanding the use of specific material culture, the considerations for academicians are only served by martial practices that have been preserved close enough to their original state to be of use in reaching scholarly goals.

What Is *Jiu Jitsu*?

Imagine for a moment that Kenjutsu, the sword discipline of the Samurai of feudal Japan, was gone, and only Kendo, its modern sportier offspring, left to preside in its place. There may be more similarities between the two than differences, but Kendo is not Kenjutsu, and the loss of the latter would be grievous culturally, martially, and historically.

Whether a martial pursuit be sporty or militant, the all-important distinction is in relation to function, and that is something that can be conveniently determined through observation alone. The vigorous competition in any sport, especially a combative one, demands the creation of a safe and controlled environment for the participants, whereas the vigorous committal to a combat discipline demands the preparation for an environment that is predetermined to be unsafe and uncontrolled.

In tournaments such as those conducted by the supporters of sport fencing, Karate, Taekwondo, Olympic wrestling, Judo and boxing, most of the modifications either happened generations ago in a half-remembered time far enough forgotten that the discipline itself recalls none of its former self in its own appearance, or the sport has a sibling still alive that more closely resembles an earlier mode, as it itself was originally in its youth. It's the latter that are the lucky ones, the former the lost. Boxing for example lives almost only as a sport, and nothing else, save for only the bare-knuckle practice. Karate has brethren that are still sharp to the touch and bright to the eye and weapons that have been maintained. Sport Fencing could almost be called lost, however a group of gentlemen in the United States, and others in Europe, that are quite distinct from any medieval reenactment society, have accomplished much work rediscovering Renaissance martial arts and the complex medieval systems of fight that they were built upon. This work has been wrought with passion and constitution and perseverance, so much so that sport fencing's ancestry has been given more than identity, but form and functionality – and has so been saved from oblivion.[8]

Considering the fates of those combat traditions which weren't fortunate enough to remain intact, whose only survival was as a sport, Jūjutsu fared relatively well. It escaped the most detrimental aspects of transformation. Only moderately scathed and bruised, the present condition of all its modern modes, while no doubt altered from their original forebear, are still capable of providing insights into the feudal archetypes they are descended from. Also its position is stronger in that the offspring range as widely from Aiki-Jūjutsu to Aikido, from Judo to Brazilian Jiu Jitsu. The lethal maneuvers are still present and functional, in the Japanese variants especially, and neither has the discipline in most cases been divorced from the sword. All these variations, combined with the discipline's native strengths and broad applicability, have created an overall stronger position in that its attracted a vast multitude of adherents and gained immeasurable celebrity and prestige. This all but guarantees a lifespan of great and unforeseeable length - even be it due to the existence of innumerable schools creating a bewildering variance of quality.

Not all other forms of fight were so fortunate: *Pankration* may have preceded Olympic wrestling, and may still even exist somewhere on the Greek mainland or the Cyclades, but cultural jewels like the *Arming Sword and Shield* methods of fight out of the Middle Ages, or the *Schiavona and Buckler* methods of the fourteenth century were very nearly lost to the present day scholar – and only now is work being carried out to retrieve them. This is to say nothing of those most ancient customs and codes of practice that came out of the Cradle of Civilization, or out of Rome itself, where weapons like the *Gladius*, despite its advantage of having played a central role in the most famous of sports arenas and having conquered the ancient world, are a lost art of a people and time whose ingenuity is still felt today.

It is a bizarre irony, that in those instances where the combat sport has no combat discipline in concurrent existence with it, and its origins are drowned in the tides of time, that it was its embracement as a sport that saved it. Even if that salvation was something regrettably less noble and glorious – perhaps not as bad as seeing a Hoplite shield being used as a saucepan – it is still something more dignifying than a flexible foil trying to retrace the patterns of the court sword with little or no link to its ancestor. In instances such as sport fencing, the ancestor is so far removed in function that it's difficult to even make a tenuous connection with the buried truth, leaving exhumation as the only means of qualifying the relationship. So many methods of sword fighting and of unarmed aggression that belonged to those eras which were portrayed in sport to entertain a nation, and as well as in anger to protect it, are now only retrievable by the literarily adept and historically inclined.

Chapter 5

Combat Sports and Combat Disciplines

At this stage the critical question of the first priority is: how does a martial art become a combat sport, intended for the ring as opposed to the battlefield?

This, as predictably expected, is a gradual affair. Usually combat sports originate from some earlier, bloodier, more violent contest that was less official, less regulated and not intended for mass marketing to the general public. In some cases this never changes, even when a combat sport becomes well established – the original contest remains unaltered. Take bare-knuckle boxing, a vicious combat that easily predates professional boxing and yet still thrives in some of the more shadowy places. Jūjutsu continued on, unaffected and itself unchanged, after the creation of Judo, or the inclusion of Judo as an Olympic sport. These two examples still exist in both original and now competition forms, whereas disciplines such as Karate, Taekwondo, Kung Fu and Muay Thai have seen a competition system set up within them, a grading mechanism for the quality of their members, with competitions now common between them as well, such as K-1 and other striking tournaments like it. In these latter cases no competition art actually arose, so much as a competition arose within the practice of the art itself, changing the discipline from the inside out. For some this impacted them little, for others it impacted them considerably. Taekwondo is a highly popular competition art, and almost specializes in the tournament format as well as having a great deal of its curriculum adapted for that sole purpose. Karate as well. For some of these martial arts there are many different styles, some focusing more on things outside the competition circuit like weaponry or street-grade tactics, some others on things within the competition circuit, such as sparring or form. There are some cases where the Jūjutsu you learn at the local *dojo* is the very same one you'll take with you onto the mat. That happens. This would be particularly true of the Brazilian variety.

However, what has become the trend is to put a fighter through precision training, to better his chances as much as may be. So coaches have emerged with their own highly respected and deeply regarded training camps, the greater the champions they've trained the more prestigious the camp. These guys tend to be at the very top of the competition fight game and use only the most exacting training regimens to develop their fighters. That means they're in the business to win, and to do so they're not about to waste an ounce of time on any part of a fighter's conditioning that doesn't contribute to his chances for success. A good example of this is the absence of weaponized tactics in MMA schools or gyms; why would they waste time with something that isn't going to contribute in reaching the goal? There is no weapon-based combat in the MMA. Not the Ultimate Fighting Championship, not Pride Fighting Championship when it existed, not in the World Vale Tudo Championships. Nothing. It wouldn't be any more irrational for an MMA camp to spend three hours a day on ping pong strategy than it would for them to invest time in edged weapon theory. When you stop and consider that their profession is about efficiency, it's not difficult to understand why any maneuver or technique or strategy that doesn't produce results is dropped in favor of those that do. The strongest attributes that MMA can be credited with are its embrace of breadth of tactics and maneuvers: its combination of professional boxing with Olympic wrestling ground control, or a Muay Thai striking element working in conjunction with a Brazilian Jiu Jitsu background. The one key characteristic of those disciplines that are brought together is that they usually represent the most practical varieties of striking and grappling methods. Boxing, kick boxing, and Muay Thai seem to be amongst the preferred modes of battering, while Jiu Jitsu, Olympic or Greco-Roman Wrestling, Sambo and Vale Tudo are amongst the preferred modes of crushing. Note, that though I list these as some of the most preferred modes, they're most definitely not the only ones.

There are two divergent opinions on the MMA model of fight (sometimes referred to as a hybrid) in that techniques from at least two disciplines are merged to produce an offspring that shares a moderate degree of similarity with both. The first is that they've traded off specialization for diversity: for example, if Judo was one contributor, the MMA approach would need only those throws and sweeps and chokes that are most practicable and tactically valid in the type of fight environment it will be used in. The needs of an MMA trainer and his camp aren't going to encompass the entire discipline of Judo obviously, but more likely will take in a percentage of it, while the rest of the material for the fighter will be composed of kickboxing. Only those punches, kicks and combinations from kickboxing that are observably most effective and most applicable are taken.

Conventional rationale would determine that either element, be it the Judo or the kickboxing, is made weaker in the absence of the material that got left behind – that lack of complete architecture – despite the new strengths found in the rounding out of the fighter's ability. It's difficult to deny that there is some truth in this, but it's bound up with another reality: the two now combined can achieve something that perhaps neither alone could before. This represents the second opinion on the hybrid combat sports within the MMA: the combination of the best techniques from two opposite styles of fight – one grappling, one striking – create something not better, but *better-suited* for the new type of fight contest that MMA represents. It is also of key importance to note that much of what was left out of hybrid fight designs were techniques unnecessary anyway due to regulations that forbid lethal maneuvers, small joint locks, tension tactics as well as certain striking practices. The advent of these combination-systems weren't specialized for application in field combat, but were specifically constructed for applications in sport combat – a trade-off that allowed not for the creation of the sport, but for its development.

The MMA emergence has proven more than entertaining in the way it's turned out, and an interesting study in development, branching away from the kind of tournaments still typical and popular in Brazil and Russia – grit minus the glamour – while the English-speaking world capitalizes on the opportunity. It's not entirely a bad thing, treating something as an enterprise-opportunity first, before treating it as a sport – the sport won't get the publicity without the marketing, and to get the marketing one needs to view everything as money and potential money. This approach isn't only responsible for the massive popularity now enjoyed by the MMA, but also the very different feel it has from the contests it started out as: the tooth and claw, rite of passage that could only be conceived and incubated, then live and breathe, in the less delicate parts of the world. If one remembers back to the 1990s, the earliest glimpse home audiences got was of an exotic life form, imported and caged, and for a very short time, uncompromisingly vicious.

The ferocity wasn't to last though, a taming was coming and it had to if the thing was going to be allowed to stay. Yet, for those seemingly few short glimpses there was something more than captivation, more than breathtaking when so many martial artists were gathered together from all over the world, drawn out of sometimes strange and unheard of disciplines, to fight without restraint. How it must have sounded to them when it was proposed to participate in a competition that would allow the full range of techniques and tactics as long as they didn't use lethality. What a way to magnetize the most dangerously skilled, proficient and intrepid men to one place with the promise of indisputable glory. To win the thing meant a man was the best, and no argument could dilute the potency of that statement.

Here was a means to test the mettle of an unarmed warrior while forbidding only the barbarous of fighters: the eye gougers, the fish hookers and the biters. Or, more precisely, not to forbid them to fight, only forbid them to give in to such instincts. It was a sobering testament to the reality of the gauntlet that had been imagined, built and soon used to sift out a victor, that things like groin strikes hadn't been added to the list of the forbidden. A chill nearly descends at the idea of such legitimacy, the knowledge that the creators of such a mechanism – as this tournament clearly was – didn't want the results attacked or debased by criticisms and accusations of a combat too controlled or whose rules were too reserved. The designers had gone about their business, tweaking and tinkering and ironing out the wrinkles to create a trial by fire, a medieval gauntlet, that forbade only the killing of the other man; and the use of the three most heinous attacks they could imagine (biting, eye-gouging and fish-hooking), things that made use of teeth and fingernails. All of this the Gracie family did to end all debate when they pushed for the acceptance of the tournament format that is now commonly referred to as MMA: silence all protest, quell the objections and declare – through action – the superiority of their family's concepts.

And at the heart of that family's concepts stood the powerful and awful animal of tremendous capability: Jūjutsu. Though Judo was the original blueprint, Judo is the direct offspring of Jūjutsu, so very close to it in substance and execution. This was the baseline model which Helio and Carlos Gracie would make their modifications to. With additions and subtractions that seem inspired more by Grecian traditions than by Japanese, but with the underlying DNA clearly the latter, a specialized subspecies was born. The system's design was evidently ultra-focused, but this fine-tuning was envisioned and carried out by men who knew that the methodology of their discipline could be made all the keener if it were even more streamlined and efficient, and so increased the martial art's reliance on leverage and position and diversion. This created an animal that could grab onto just about any other animal in the jungle and maul it indefinitely. It wasn't that the Jiu Jitsu the Gracies had idealized was something uniquely new, but rather had taken something already extremely effective and isolated and identified those characteristics that made it effective and magnified their operation throughout the system, which created a predator that naturally sought the ground as its preferred environment of operation.

This animal, now genetically engineered to the designer's specifications, was ready to loose onto a fight scene that Brazil today owes so much of its popularity to: in the earlier part of the twentieth century, no doubt especially from the 1930s to 1980s, Brazil fostered a fight environment between Luta Livre and Brazilian Jiu Jitsu that created tournaments – and conditions in general – that produced very hardened and steely fighters. Whether a Brazilian fighter supports Luta Livre, Vale Tudo or Jiu Jitsu in the end, the work the Gracie family did put Brazil's fight traditions on the international stage and cannot be overlooked, as it benefits all the modes of fight coming out of that country.

That first Ultimate Fighting Championship was a tournament specifically modeled to mimic, as close as reasonably possible, the conditions found in a semi-controlled environment – making allowances for the absence of arms and lethality – but making it general knowledge that everything else was on the table. This, the tournament designers must have known, was the very closest that they would ever get it to resemble Brazil's tournaments and even this had been hard to bring to pass. One must wonder whether or not the designers and promoters and investors knew the format was doomed, unable to stave off its own implosion, the vacuum destined to be filled by a format more familiar to the target audience. Who knows? What we do know is that the statement they made, that of their martial art system's superiority in nearly unrestricted competition (and again a parallel statement of the superiority of their nation's tournament model) was made and heard. It could not be called 'an experiment', that first UFC, because it wasn't. The Brazilians knew what they were creating in terms of a tournament format and knew that the formula worked. They had imported it after all. It was definitely a statement. They beat everyone. And very soon after the beginning of these tournaments, the only disciplines close to rivaling them were those that used a similar specialization in maneuvers and tactics, what could be called a singularly-focused methodology. But even when they were beaten by other competitors in the tournaments they'd popularized, a long way down the road, it was with the lessons that they themselves had taught the world at large to use. The last smile was still theirs. Helio and Carlos certainly would have smiled at the impact of their creation.

The men that arrived in the United States to compete in that very first tournament were some of the best in the world at their respective disciplines, some at the leading edge of skill and conditioning. So many world class fighters converged in that initial contest, and an elimination one at that, where a fighter would have to fight numerous times before the evening expired, and all of them having disciplines so clearly distinct from one another. And even more than being distinct from one another was that even types of fight that were closely related in combat methodology – shoot fighting and Jiu Jitsu or kickboxing and Karate – would approach the road to victory with sometimes entirely different mindsets, battle plans and tactics.

When you take into account what these competitors are up against in the quality of their opponents and the immense task of rising to the top through a quagmire of fierce opposition, it's easy to understand a training plan that rejects any less than effective technique, or rejects a fighter who has a penchant for employing any technique outside of regulations and risks being disqualified. A fighter who unintentionally uses illegal tactics (especially in the early years of these tournaments, before there was training camps), may very well have only acted reflexively, using maneuvers that while not allowable in the tournament were techniques all the same that had been practiced until they were instinct. This would be the direct result of prior combat training in something not only more lethal, but in all likelihood something unfamiliar with the concept of regulatory governance. These reflexes, if incompatible with a new combat pursuit, like one that requires a transition from a full contact school to a low contact school, may just not be easily possible. This type of physiological indoctrination, such as it is, has taught the anatomy to almost act autonomously – trying to un-teach it may be more trouble than its worth, and too time-expensive. This is also the underlying reason it's unwise to undertake the learning of two martial arts that are dissimilar from one another: it only serves to send the mind and body conflicting signals, lessons, priorities and methods.

There is an erroneous belief that reflex conditioning, that combat indoctrination mentioned above that allows the anatomy to almost act autonomously, can be altered at will and on a whim. It is a belief often held by the uninitiated, but not the unschooled, and one that is quite insupportable and even threatening to oneself - which makes the following account so very odd. A good friend of mine had been trained in a highly fluid striking system, but at low contact for the sake of being able to compete and win (without disqualification) on the tournament circuit. Once in conversation he confided that he viewed a street fight as a full contact sparring match; and because he was schooled to strike at low-contact, a thing unsuitable for a real fight, he declared that it was easily solved by employing heavier striking power and treating his attacker like a *full-contact* sparring partner. It sounds good on the surface – right somehow – but it isn't. It isn't right because the implication is that there is a switch that can be flipped, and low contact becomes full contact....with the same speed and efficiency. It's the end that's false. The switch exists, and can be consciously flipped, and a person can 'choose' to hit harder than what is presently practiced. The worst self-deceptions are those that are half-true. The problem with his thinking was his reflex-conditioning was at low contact. His body had reflex speed only at low contact; full contact was slowed down by slower-than-reflex conscious choice. Martial art masters and philosophers have long said, "Anything less than reflex speed is too slow." Such will always be the case. It's night and day. You are what you train, what you tell yourself, and what you program yourself or your body to be. In regard to that friend, he eventually changed his views after meeting someone who'd trained in nothing but full contact. This had happened in the other guy's *dojo*, so despite the fact that it was full contact, the environment they fought in was a controlled one: a ring, mats, first aid kits and first aid certificate holders, and onlookers who bore a responsibility for inaction if things should spiral out of what was reasonably acceptable. The low-contact fighter, the friend in question, limped out at the end of the sparring session, having been beaten competitively and bodily by the full contact fighter. He flipped the figurative switch to go from low contact to full, but lost reflex speed as a result. The other guy didn't suffer any such handicap: he trained full contact all the time and struck for full force at reflex speed - and won. True story.

Despite all that grief and embarrassment, things could have been considerably worse: they could have ended up in a similar debate outside the *dojo*, after a few drinks at a bar... And that fast we go from the controlled environment where the 'sparring' happened, to a hypothetical uncontrolled environment where it would have been a fight. Both these guys involved were sportsmen, career competitors, and both understood the value of restraint, to say nothing of the 'devices of restraint' that are typically found in combat sports: authorities greater than the combatants and all manner of other professionals. An uncontrolled environment has no audience, no referees, no peers, certainly no doctors on standby, no cut-men, no timed rounds, no one to throw a towel and admit surrender on someone's behalf, not so much as a first aid kit or reassurance of any kind. That's the difference: competition is regulated. It's ruled. It's carefully crafted to be as safe as they can manage to make it, because the end goal is to beat the other guy, not kill him.

Combat disciplines are not controlled. They are what would be considered field tactics and they are used in uncontrolled environments in life and death scenarios – battlefield conditions. To appreciate a combat discipline's unreserved approach to the ugliest of tactical scenarios, one must imagine those physical attributes so common amongst martial artists: the eye-blink speed of a jab, the deft dexterity to put oneself behind an opponent to attack from the back, the unconventional vectoring and narrow impact strikes such as chops, reverse chops and ridge hands, knowledge of the anatomy's arterial system...

Let us now entertain the idea that the blink-fast jab isn't actually a jab...it's still firing straight off the shoulder, but now the hand is open and the extended fingers add an extra three inches of reach and close the distance that much sooner, not targeting the face, but the eyes in that face. Not possible? A technique repeated a few hundred times a day, even if only three days out of every seven, is six hundred times a week for however many years the martial artist has decided to invest in it. In only a year the martial artist has practiced this attack over thirty thousand times. He's probably conditioned his fingers using sand or some other material for resistance to strengthen them for just this purpose. The best angles and best diversions have been calculated long ahead of time. It's more than possible he's going to blind his opponent, it's closer to likely – and if he can generate any element of surprise whatsoever, the chances are going to be farther from *likely* and closer to *certainly*. We needn't explore this line of thought much further, only to imagine that the person struck is temporarily blinded, falling back fast and squinting, groping to cover their eyeballs. They can't see. Their attacker can. This is over.

Practicing martial artists are usually familiar with that intense urgency that is accompanied by a characteristic crushing force which comes right after your opponent has arrived behind you, positioning themselves for the application of a choke-hold. The dexterity and understanding of displacements needed to be able to achieve this position are dangerous because of the likelihood of choking maneuvers...but what if the adversary isn't choking? He begins what feels like a choke-hold, but then redistributes his weight through a shift of the hips, preparing for a violent twist – a concerted effort of upper and lower body – with the intent of separating the cervical vertebrae, snapping the neck. True, a choke-hold would've rendered the opponent unconscious in a minute or so, but then, that is a whole minute that the person caught still has to struggle, and if they're schooled well in their own discipline they may be able to make the sixty seconds of consciousness pay off and work to a better position. Not so if the attacker's aim is to break the neck at first opportunity. Popular belief is that any twist will accomplish such a maneuver, but this like all other modern fairy tales is an overstatement. There is technique to the accomplishment of the maneuver, and not every combat discipline practices it – let alone many combat sports that have no direct or professional need for it.

Across disciplines like Taekwondo, Karate, Tangsoodo and Kung Fu are striking techniques that use the anatomy's natural edges in cutting motions, such as the hand blade (from the pinky finger to the base of the palm, which is used during *chops*) or on the opposite side of the hand from the index finger's tip to the wrist (after having tucked the thumb against the palm, which is used during *ridge hands*). These are used everywhere in combat sports, though not a great deal within MMA, but in venues that favor competition between striking disciplines. They are consistently employed for use in breaking techniques, whether that of stacked wood or brick. In the arsenal of a combat discipline they are instrumental in a completely different capacity: when used from a perpendicular position they can be practiced against targets like the trachea, which takes little force to lethally crush, or against the upper spine. Regardless of how it appears to the reader, one has to understand that practiced every day until made reflexive, these maneuvers when in the opening stages of an engagement, or during a moment of ideal execution, can not only win but potentially kill or maim. It represents what can be done with tools outside of the sportsman rivalry mindset, and in one of need and last resort.

Many combat sports have a number of choke-holds in their toolbox, some of which, as most of us know, create asphyxiation and others blood-flow obstruction, but not all martial artists or competitors know or need to know why a blood-choke works, only how to apply it correctly from any number of positions. The difference between the grittiest combat disciplines and everything else (many combat sports included) is important to take into full account. Many combat disciplines, Japanese Jūjutsu being one, will not only educate their students as to the identification of the arteries and where they are, but how they should be optimally attacked. This will make a world of difference for the student, because knowledge of location and function and disruption can allow him to attack using teeth, nails and anything else; the damage done by even a cleaving hand strike such as a ridge hand to the jugular can drop a person at the least, incapacitate them at best.[9]

What Is *Jiu Jitsu*?

In just these four examples - the jab's mechanics turned into an eye-gouge; the choke turned into an attack on the vertebrae; cutting strikes applied to vital points as opposed to non-critical targets; arteries made targetable as opposed to being afforded exemption - we can see what kind of alteration takes place in potential outcome when knowledge, training practices, technique character or even mindset changes to include the most extreme applications available to the imagination. It should be noted that these four comparisons stated do not take weaponry into account. Each example when considered in light of weaponized techniques takes on a whole other impact and consideration, types of attack that simply aren't possible within sanctioned competition anywhere. The startling poignancy of the contrast begins to become apparent with but a handful of examples, then broadens out when one considers that many traditional disciplines still include weaponry in their repertoire: Jūjutsu, Aiki-Jūjutsu, Aikido, and Ninjutsu will in many cases teach some form of Japanese sword; every other style of Karate will teach some form of *Kobudo* (weaponry) that includes everything from *Sais* to *Kamas* to *Tonfas* to *Bo* staffs to *Nunchakus*; Kung Fu have their swords and spears as do many Korean disciplines; and Filipino martial arts are renowned for their understanding of edged weapons, knives especially. With the unrestricted usage of combat maneuvers as described above, empowered to be as lethal as need dictates, then combined with the use of blunt and edged weapons, schooling for situations such as mass attack scenarios (multiple assailants) becomes far more effective. Nor is it uncommon in a combat discipline to be taught tactics explicitly designed to thwart life-threatening attacks with a lethal counterattack.

The same skills of any martial artist, professional competitor or field combatant, cross over between the lethal and non-lethal techniques, but the difference is that only field combatants actually practice with a full range of lethal maneuvers, ignoring none. That being said a great many techniques in the realm of professional competition become lethal with only a change in the mindset of the martial artist – a choke held a little too long, one too many punches, kicks or other strikes delivered from the mount, a crucifix maneuver from the arsenal of Brazilian Jiu Jitsu and so on. The maneuvers outside of competition tend to more often be critical from the outset in their objective, whereas in competition it's not only not necessary, but not desirable. Ultimately this all must be placed in careful perspective by the prospective student, so that no time is wasted with a training platform that doesn't meet the needs of the participant.

Taking those attributes that make competition techniques so awe-inspiring and mesmerizing to watch and moving them into a situation more desperate and mode of attack far more lethal does give pause for thought. Take the same speed, blindsiding, power of momentum or leverage or kinetic linking, of diversion and distraction, of torsion and torque, assigning new weapons and targets to each principle and a whole other plateau of destruction is reached, one that snuffs life out like candles.

The memory of attendance at those schools during youth is a balance of ferocious tactics set against ferocious discipline concerning behavioral conduct: safety was non-negotiable, and anyone caught not practicing safely (as much as was possible given the curriculum) was dealt with severely. Tolerances were nil. It wasn't the type of place, or administered by the type of personalities, that would ever be susceptible to that brand of whining and mewling that is now regularly used to relax standards. If someone couldn't comply, for whatever reason, then they departed. This molding process, which in many ways is not alienated from the discipline found in modern soldiery, is a sobering awakening, and not an unwelcome one. As people are eliminated due to incompatibility, what is left by way of this natural weeding method is only the determined...who are not yet strong or hard or fast or dangerous, but who have a chance to be.

They're taught to come as close to the breaking point of a joint lock, or the wrenching point of a torque, not for fear that they may pass it and damage their training partner (though it does serve this purpose incidentally), but so that they'll know 'how' and 'where' to pass it when, and God forbid 'if', the time should ever come. The situations that had been envisioned for the use of such violent answers are prepared for with a 'worst case scenario' mentality – always assuming that a submission hold will not suffice and that a bleaker and harsher dialogue will be required. In many Jūjutsu schools the white belt rank exposes the student to an introduction calculated to prime them for the unforgiving severity of the program ahead, and by doing so not only filters out those who cannot proceed from those who can, but also creates unflinching, steely martial artists.

So if you are looking at Jūjutsu and want to study it, and wondering what you should pursue, a Combat Discipline or a Combat Sport, you should really ask yourself what you want from it. If you think you'd like to compete in amateur MMA and perhaps pour your heart into professional MMA, then you probably need a gym or camp specializing in MMA, as anything other than that will waste your time. This is difficult because every school under the sun claims the MMA education experience is available through them. This has been seen more times than can be counted; and not one of which I've personally seen do I actually believe was genuinely experienced in what they were marketing. MMA is a type of fight that requires specialized instruction, not just any instruction. If you want to learn techniques and tactics not usable within the confines of tournament fighting, lethal maneuvers and ancient weapons, then you should steer towards the traditional *dojos*. MMA schools can provide a combat education that you can carry into the street and fight with, and win with, the same as a traditional school can provide you with the techniques to take to a tournament, but neither of these can do the other's job anywhere near as well as its counterpart can. This is imperative to know and remember.

It isn't every traditional *dojo* that offers the uncompromising brutality described above but the schools this writer attended did because the schools with these traits were the ones that were sought for. There were many along the way that didn't offer that kind of instruction, but offered quality nonetheless, just minus the commitment to preparation for the worst case scenario – these were rejected for personal reasons. As I said, it wholly depends on what the reader is searching for. If you know ahead of time what that is, then the search is all the easier. It's when you're not sure that it becomes complicated. There are Jūjutsu schools that have a much more temperate approach. If this is what you seek, then be encouraged because there are many competent schools that are actually trying to attract students as oppose to frighten them away (I say this because the schools I chose were plagued with rock bottom student enrollment due to the severity of the training regimens followed).

There is also survivability to consider, and not just yours, but the school's. Many schools open and close in modestly sized cities; many more open and close and open again, in the same city. Others move and shift, from place to place, tied to the financial misfortunes of their owners. Think about all this. It would be prudent to choose a school that has either been standing for a while and whose continued existence is somewhat reliable, or one that in some way has given you reason to believe it's here to stay. The repercussion is that if you choose a school that closes its doors ten months down the road (this has been personally experienced) and you have to relocate to another school, you run the real risk of the material you learned having infrequent incompatibilities to outright alienation with the new school. It could be even worse (and this has happened too), you may find no other school of the kind that just closed on you. And there wouldn't be a thing you could do about it. This kind of seismic instability concerning the landscape of martial art schools isn't made common knowledge nearly often enough or maybe it's different in other places where they are far more stable and profitable and dependable. From all this writer has read, and seen, and been told by colleagues, it's for the most part shifty and precarious everywhere you go. There will always be those schools that are being managed like a business and not a *dojo*, so they exist as a livelihood for the person who owns it, and it'll be tied to the financial talents of its owner to stay open and continue the provision of service or be another empty rental space. But even when a school is found whose existence is more assured than most others, the next question presents itself naturally: are they teaching the discipline you want to learn.[10] Sometimes, in order to attempt profitability, three or four instructors from different disciplines will share one *dojo* and try to make it succeed that way. And half the time they'll close too. For most instructors teaching doesn't make a good livelihood, but it does make a great pastime and lifestyle, and so for those that teach out of passion and aren't depending on the school to eat, live and satisfy their financial obligations, their schools tend to survive better – because the owner's bills at home are paid by better occupations than teaching. There was a Jūjutsu master in my hometown who taught not because he had to, but because he wanted to. He had an occupation and it wasn't related to martial arts. The last I heard, twenty years later, his dojo still stands.

Chapter 6

Combat System Architecture

A martial art's architecture is not only the quantity of material that it encompasses, but also how that material has been brought together in relationship to each other and why. The thinking responsible for design, the mind that oversaw the initial decisions of what should be included and what should be omitted, ultimately determined the shape and feel of the system being looked at, even if it didn't create the need that demanded the construction.

The obvious assumption concerning any 'need' for a combat system is that the need can be simplified, reduced to nothing more than a generalized means for defense. However this would represent a gross misunderstanding of the widely varying threats, and the distinct needs they create, on a medieval battlefield...but everywhere else as well.

To defend oneself in an individualistic capacity, from tactics used person to person, armed or unarmed, in many ways works upon the same principle as the needs of a feudal lord or his appointed general to counter anything as broad in scope as enemy archery or infantry or cavalry, on a wide field of battle. This is to simply say that whether the preparation is of one soldier to fight against another soldier, empty handed or not, it'll require the same kind of analytical thinking, systematic construction and process-based implementation as preparing a whole regiment to counter the tactics of an opposing regiment. As a swordsman would require a different defensive attitude and techniques as opposed to a spearman, so would an unarmed soldier need specialized training and tactics to fight either of them without having the benefit of a weapon himself.

These types of examples could go on and on into the unforeseeable future.

The needs of any battlefield, quite regardless of era, nation or location, would be dauntingly varied without any compounding factors such as the introduction of a new means, a new belligerent, new environmental conditions or new philosophical or metaphysical motivations. A major motivator in the use of Jūjutsu, as well as the creation of it, was the need to address the dilemma of having to fight unequipped, or having been made so by unpreventable disarmament. If a member of a general's elite troops was suddenly relegated to the ranks of the unarmed, under-equipped and there was no hope of rearmament, a valuable asset stood to be lost: not only the soldier's life obviously but the general's confidence that the incident was an isolated occurrence. Jūjutsu and Aiki-Jūjutsu were designed to fight unarmed, utilized in the event of disarmament, but most importantly to prevent disarmament.

Though every situation on a battlefield had highly precise needs that required a highly precise systematic reaction, what can be generalized are the guiding principles used to outline the construction of most, if not all, martial arts. The first and probably most important of these guiding principles is that which governs the correlation between *combat system needs* and *anatomical limitations*. It would be unheard of to prescribe a tactical solution, a maneuver, that required the movement of the body in a way that couldn't be done in a given scenario. Such a fallibility would have become obvious during the first attempt in the practice yard, and so discarded. The actual danger would have been in prescribing a maneuver to answer an attack that required the anatomy to move in a way not impossible, but not entirely natural. If it sounds like this would constitute careless construction policy on behalf of the system designer, it's because it does. It may also seem apparent that such designs were necessarily overhauled to eliminate anything that could potentially become problematic, but this was not a pervasive truth: they might have been, but the ill-conceived components may have been added far later. Here and there, though they be a real rarity, particular mandated movements of anatomy during certain exercises slipped through. While these movements weren't necessarily working against the anatomy, they were still too close to a decidedly antagonistic range of motion, in which the likelihood of accumulative stress was simply too great to permit it to remain a part of the larger framework.

These instances, once detected, are easily corrected. In present experience they tended to affect joints and the range of the relative limb more than anything else. A theory on these elaborate and unneeded attachments (such as they were) is that as the systems in question fell out of mainstream usage and became the instrument of public education, catering to the more ordinary, the disciplines – as said already - degraded from lack of routine field testing that the battlefield so conveniently supplied. The result was an attitude that year by year, decade by decade, grew ever more concerned with performing the operating principle within a technique than actually demonstrating the operability of the technique itself. This leads to a systematic failure wherein a technique's principle is functional and good, but the application of that principle (the actual method of use) is dysfunctional and poor. It's shockingly simple for a principle to be employed in a substandard technique and instantly made worthless. While not exactly common, it's nowhere near uncommon enough for comfort. This has personally been encountered across a range of systems, upwards to five different arts of Japanese and Korean origin (which means nothing, because this malpractice is everywhere), within both grappling and striking types. The anatomical range of motion violations, the negligent misuse of combat principles in decrepit techniques, the amateur usage of striking tactics in grappling systems (and grappling tactics in striking systems), all highlights dangerous shortcomings in modern system architectures.

Design ultimately must conform firstly to anatomical limitations; secondly to assessed need; thirdly to efficient use of principle in the construction of maneuvers; and fourthly must place emphasis on tactical operation of maneuvers, not on demonstration of principles that such maneuvers use. This doesn't cover the entirety of common design flaws, but as far as this chapter has gone, this list has so far brought attention to the first four failings and in correct order of priority.

The danger of design flaws through degradation is something that affects combat disciplines far more than combat sports, this being because the modernization required to restore optimum operation has already been applied to the disciplines from which many of the combat sports drew their techniques from. The combat disciplines in most dire need of attention are those that have succeeded their antiquated forerunners, but received no attention, or correction, in the realm of uncontrolled environments, and hence whose functionality is best suited for the *dojo* where practice entails little risk. I don't think these martial arts that have survived should be discontinued or lost, and have already stated the cultural and historical value of these arts. Yet the prospective student must exercise diligence and wariness when selecting a course of study in the combat sciences – most of us are looking for modernized variants, with working techniques that can be applied under duress and complicated conditions. One excellent way to determine if the discipline you're looking at suits your needs is to imagine, then write down, ten of your most pressing questions that concern you regarding the positions you may find yourself in during an attack. Next ask someone from the school you're looking at to show you their solutions for the ten queries you've written down - then see if the answers you're given convince you of their viability. You shouldn't use this method alone for determining the school, but it's definitely an irreproachable place to start.

System Components

Almost every combat discipline today is descended from an older tradition, some ancient and some less so. This means that the greater majority of disciplines currently in use have undergone development periods for scores upon scores of years, many in excess of centuries, if not *millennia*. For any process like a martial art system to experience advancement throughout such lengthy durations as in the case of centuries or tens of centuries, the potential yield could be colossal advantages in terms of purgation or refinement (admittedly, there would also be the contrary effect as well to contend with, which has already been covered in the section on degradation).

Thought of like this, the construction process of just about any martial art functioning today cannot, or only in a very limited way, be of any assistance in our consideration of their construction – simply because too much change has occurred for most of these disciplines, good or bad, to cast any light on their designs in the beginning. Yet, if one looks hard enough an example or two can be found, from *Krav Maga* to *Pancrase*. Another modern example, and of superb system design, is an outstanding specimen called Sambo: a Russian martial art created in the earlier part of the twentieth century.

самозащита без оружия

SAMozashchita Bez Oruzhiya

SELF DEFENSE WITHOUT WEAPONS

SAMBO

Sambo, or *SAMozashchita Bez Oruzhiya*, literally means Self Defense Without Weapons. An effective and powerful system of fight, Sambo has attained global popularity, a fame completely deserved. It represents a young discipline brought together in relatively recent history from slow and patient study in the Union of Soviet Socialist Republics (USSR), the approach to its construction every ounce as methodical as the system is itself. The research that would help to largely form and characterize it stretched out across countries and continents, searching out the most useful maneuvers from many modes of fight, and then adopting and combining them around a distinctly Russian core system. The approach to the construction, from the gathering of materials to the assembly and quality control processes, to the education of the early teachers is a solid and unassailable example of how such an enormous goal – to create a viable, all-condition, empty-hand combat system applicable in warfare – should be envisioned-to-realized. Today the system, especially Combat Sambo, is regarded as immensely effective, sharing attributes with many of those sources it was built from, not least of which was Jūjutsu.

Just as Sambo's design reflects a certain character that in turn is a manifestation of the specifications that predominated its assembly, like *Krav Maga* and *Pancrase* after it, so does Jūjutsu's, though far older and longer in its advancement.

What Is *Jiu Jitsu*?

As you'd expect a martial art's techniques are determined by the assessed need. Imagine the need has already been typified by a repeated observation: we'll imagine that once fighting unarmed has begun, our troops consistently close distance with their enemies, strike clumsily using open hands and fists, then find themselves caught up in a protracted struggle thereafter, each having firmly seized the other, neither able to capitalize upon any advantage. The encounter ends this way, upon the feet, upon the knees and upon the ground without any way to predict who will prevail. All of it, the entire struggle, is reduced almost entirely to blind luck.

This then is established regarding the need we have: the system of fight must be able to strike much more effectively upon entering effective range (range of our limbs), using all the body's striking weapons, not only the hands – feet, knees and elbows; then, knowing a locked struggle is about to ensue the system must be able to excel to meet the situation's demands and be able to give us control over the enemy's attempts to push us over or pull us down. Now, recognizing that the exchange of strikes between them and us transitions into a clinched struggle shortly after the first blows are launched we'll allocate one fifth – 20 percent – of the system to provide us striking superiority in the opening dialogue (after all, we know the enemy had proved no more efficient than we when it came to striking). Three fifths – or sixty percent – will be allocated to that part of the fight that seems to develop quickly off the beginning, the clinched struggle, and so will be made up of grappling tactics. The last twenty percent will be invested in body conditioning.

For the benefit of the reader we'll briefly index what will roughly be included to sharpen clarity and perspective. Body conditioning will include preventive preparation which will include a joint warm up, the maintenance of a suitable training area that can absorb the weight of a falling person without imparting injury to them, maintenance of a 'practice clothing' that will reduce friction and tearing forces on the epidermis while providing absorption for perspiration – this will help in minimizing needless skin damage from friction as well as providing a place for the trainees to clinch or grab onto. Given that the assessed need is against clothed and even armored opponents, the training regimen must mimic the conditions as closely as possible. The last safety protocol instituted will be the design of five to ten (or more) deliberate falls, each made so that when a particular throw, sweep or attack is executed, the person falling can do so without risk of injury; in theory this practice will reduce our faction's injuries in actual combat if the enemy should employ similar throws, and simultaneously will allow our trainees to attack their training partners forcefully as they would in battle conditions. These 'break falls' will also be considered a part of the conditioning exercises as it hardens the student, mind and body, to being thrown. Within the scope of conditioning we will also list cardiovascular focus, for heart and lung capacity to create stamina; reflex training to provide the desired response speed to attack; stretching to reduce the likelihood of pulls or tears in the musculature, and to allow for greater range of motion, especially for leg attacks during kicking techniques. Different techniques require different postures for best results, so posturing and the use of stances will also be a part of conditioning, the goal being to instinctively know which to favor and when, and to be able to do so at reflex speed.

There are more elements than this, but here we will conclude the conditioning practices and move on to what comes next: the core system, our grappling tactics. To come to any wisdom on what will be needed to make the system functional and able to meet the demands we have for it, will require us to carefully make a survey of what kind of threats it'll face. As noted above, the hypothetical assessment indicated a grappling situation developed early in the engagement, after a striking exchange, and saw neither side able to make a decisive gain. The first tactics developed then are to break this stalemate and give us the advantage. To do this we will need maneuvers usable from a standing posture and while gripped with an opponent whose also standing square on to us. From here will be added leg reaps, inside and outside, a hip toss, a leg sweep and a balance breaker. Now each of the added maneuvers is observed in traction between two trainees, one instructed to attack and the other to defend using the chosen tactics, to determine the likelihood of success for each. They all perform adequately enough to keep in use. Now the position that results from both a successful throw and an unsuccessful throw are noted. In what positions we and the opponent end in, both after the successful throw and after the failed throw, are addressed next.

This means that the next tactics will be determined from two positions: the first from an assumption that the new throws and sweeps succeeded and created a new situation, the second from an assumption that the new throws and sweeps didn't work and the original position is still valid or has changed only slightly with the foe's reaction. The next two techniques added to the curriculum will then be firstly the follow-up of a successful attack and then the compensation for a failed one. The follow-up on a successful throw will assume a certain position and the next technique added will be one to work from that position. The compensation for a botched attack will allow for another, preferably unpredictable, maneuver.

This is a quite rough approximation of the beginning of a systematic thought process used to understand the structural envisioning of a martial art, starting with an assessment of need, then an application of acceptable solutions, further envisioned to both fail and succeed: this latest failure and success becomes the new assessment of need. This process is continued until the opponent's possible responses and positions are exhausted. This is an admittedly overly simplistic glimpse of the modeling that would be possibly used. For example even the addition of the striking material mentioned above, twenty percent worth, would have added a depth of possibilities to this equation that simply are not there at present. From the clinched struggle we assume a throw or sweep to the ground, but what if the other combatant, through schooling of his own, good fortune or training of a non-combative nature, is able to stay upright despite our most earnest attempts?

Now is introduced a need for those ranged attacks that happen with close-quarters, very close range strikes such as elbows and knees and hook punches. Consider though what a best-range striking ability – round kicks, push kicks and side kicks, paired with linear punches and chops – would have been capable of if used from the outset, especially if they would have allowed us to achieve a striking-superiority. The grapple may be unavoidable but these softening tactics that strike hard and fast at the foe before the clinch and during the clinch are immensely valuable, and may in some cases stand between success and defeat. Once we stop and imagine our system construction has been adopted by the enemy on the other side, and he's using the same or similar methodology for attack and defense, the situation complicates exponentially. Of course in the hypothetical construction of the combat system a thorough designer assumes that very thing, and the first moves can equally be an attack upon us as it could be us upon them, and for this reason a short series of guards, checks, deflections and blocks are combined with evasive displacements to properly equip the trainee with the tools to thwart and if possible counter the opponent's attacks. It's now rapidly becoming a chess match.

The system designer also needn't limit himself to reactive thinking, building and assigning maneuvers to the enemy's various positions and actions, but could also adopt a proactive approach and assign attacks that force the enemy to adopt positions advantageous to us – perhaps ones that limit his ability to use tactics he's adept in, or even place him in positions that allow us to launch far more devastating assaults than what would have been possible to begin with.

The more imaginative reader will also be quick to conclude that any change to the enemy's systems of attack and defense will necessitate a change to our own, as any change to our own system will equally force him to adapt to us – an ongoing, never ending, teeter-totter of move and counter move. But before any of this systematic design and construction can begin, first the needed techniques must exist, and then the needed tactics must be created that use those techniques. Any martial art is a system comprised of many different techniques acting in close coordination. It's one thing to say that we will need this throw, that sweep, this hip toss and that bone lock for the opening position of the engagement, but what if any one of those techniques are not enough to achieve the desired end. With those maneuvers just mentioned the system designer has the beginning of a solution, but its lacking just enough so as to be insufficient for the need. It's now realized that the solving of these tactical needs requires some vital modification to an existing technique to facilitate the needed outcome.

Put like this, the task before us begins to not only take shape in terms of complexity, but enormity. Naturally for a project with this kind of scope, the creation of a maneuver-system and its attendant tactics would require a profound knowledge and experience in the required field of study before we could even begin conceptualization, and for this reason the greatest martial arts in the world today have a long history that stretches out behind them, many of their creators having based their work on the proverbial shoulders of giants.

Techniques and Types

The construction of an actual technique can be determined in much the same way as the system's needs: observe the combative situation in question, isolate the chief complication to our position in this conflict, then begin to search for available principles that could possibly counter the enemy's action. Each technique found in a martial art is a combination of elements, from the primary principles (the combat principle that will be applied, whether a lift, a sweep, a strike, a choke etc.) to the support elements such as guards and deflections, displacements (footwork) and diversionary attacks that assist the main attack. Modify generally means to augment a technique by adding other elements to it (or subtracting or substituting), and this act is the beginning of maneuver construction. Just about all martial arts, regardless of origin, share this systematic trait. An excellent way to delineate this is by taking a simple form of attack such as a right hand punch and imagining the most basic counter move that could be made to answer it. The first thing to be taught in most martial art schools is a standard guard or block to check the incoming fist.

The second thing taught would be how to execute a form-accurate punch for the necessary generation of power, and then it would be paired with your first guard and you'd have your very first counter move. A technique of minimal design is what we're seeing here – an answer as small as possible. There are two basic principles, one blocking and one striking, to create a counter-strike technique. Some people would say that a greater minimalism can be reached than even this: remove the block and use only the punch, ensure the student isn't hit by having them move slightly out of alignment with the incoming punch and then return the counter punch. That approach, however, while viable would still have two elements, because now instead of a block we're using a displacement of the body with a little subtle footwork. This minimal state uses as few moves as possible to create an answer to the combat problem. This in many schools is how the learning process begins, by seeing these components work alone, and then gradually as the student learns and masters them they're combined to form more complex maneuvers.

Complexity doesn't mean better, however. There is a style and elegance in using techniques in small configurations (possessing few elements) that allows for an amazing adaptability. This ability to rapidly adapt is made harder when maneuvers are set in complex patterns and always practiced the same way. This is training hall law: the longer something is practiced the more engraved it becomes – reflex-reactions – psychologically and physiologically. The mind begins to see the maneuvers, first and foremost, in the form they're practiced. They're practiced so long like that (thousands upon thousands of times) that your body's muscle memory begins to do it on autopilot, and in a fight you reflexively answer with the technique as it was learned and practiced. You can of course choose to alter, modify or otherwise change the technique to meet your particular situation's needs, but the changes won't be at reflex speed but much slower. This must be remembered.

As one might already suspect there is a certain speed that comes from leaving the maneuver in a complex form that guarantees it can be carried out with a speed greater than what would have otherwise been possible, and this rapidity might be the very thing that allows the technique not only to succeed, but accomplishes the kind of dominance sought for, the kind necessary for victory. So which way to go? Small compact maneuvers that don't look beyond the immediate need and are highly configurable allow the student to more easily change with the fluctuations of each new second, and having been purposely introduced and practiced that way are proven during activities such as sparring – the ever-changing nature of sparring being similar to actual engagement. In striking schools the practice of sparring is a beautiful exercise of constant improvisation, like water always moving and forcing the participants to push the limits of martial creativity with whatever skills they have. The more daringly complex techniques work opposite to this, however, and rely on set patterns that do not change, or if they do, only but a little. The difficulty is in having high adaptability while attempting to maintain long fixed form maneuvers. Many traditional schools, not only Jūjutsu, will try to balance this. And even sparring itself isn't always the promotion of power and skill it should be, but rather depends on how it is being practiced. It will certainly teach the body reflexivity, but if it's happening at low contact then the body will strike automatically at low contact once the long conditioning is complete. This is fine if it's not intended for field use, but using something like low contact striking in a fight is harder than first imagined: the body instinctively wants to strike with highly controlled and tempered force – and in the street that's a no-no.

The more complex maneuvers, usually practiced at full force (fixed forms similar to kata, but far shorter), are usually applied wholeheartedly, usually during shadow practice (solo practice) or with a classmate versed in the exact attack the complex maneuver is designed to thwart. In this regard, with little room for deviation, they are in truth very nearly opposite to the adaptable small techniques used in sparring. This means that those complex fixed forms must possess highly sound design and an inherent applicability because they cannot accommodate any deviation from the attack they're designed to counter. Their benefit lies in the unanswerable speed with which they can execute a complicated series of deft actions, a speed seemingly greater than their complexity should allow.

Regardless of technique length or complexity, elements that comprise a combat technique should always naturally complement one another, working seamlessly and cooperatively to accomplish the same thing: a highly specific result. If a technique uses a hip toss to throw an offender over and onto the ground in front of us, the use of a cross mount or full mount would now seem especially congruent, given that the hip toss provided us with ideal positioning. It stands to reason that the very next move should build upon what has been accomplished thus far. So then to group certain principles or components that already have a correlation through traits or complementary movement or action should be a predictable outcome; it is this grouping, this progression of well-matched cogs and gears, that makes combat techniques work. From that same full mounted position it's not difficult to imagine a series of punches or strikes winning the engagement: here is a common and respectable technique, long used by various systems of fight, one that neatly achieves a promising and superior ground position.

The design rule when evaluating a technique is whether or not all its components are operating in unison, contributing to an outcome in a way that amplifies the effects of one another, and that they're all doing it efficiently in the best time possible and not wasting any movement on anything less than what's absolutely necessary. Speed is what will win the day, because the faster we move the farther behind us falls the enemy's reaction time, and with his reaction not yet in motion his resistance is for a brief instant without any real strength or commitment behind it. Techniques that are of minimal moves have the advantage of succinct application due to being small, and are especially powerful in predicaments where more than one opponent is attacking and time is weighed heavily against us – survival would depend on quickly moving from assailant to assailant, and just as quickly achieving disablement or dispatch.

The drawback to this minimalist approach is that certain elements that harmonize well together and increase the power of a technique might require two or three moves; without building and practicing the technique that way, three moves happening in series, its reflex speed is still existent but on a piece-by-piece level, each move is at reflex speed, but the whole string of moves is less fast than if they'd been practiced altogether, all the time. From this perspective the rate of implementation (or attack speed) and degree of infliction (injuries to the opponent), create a kind of speed-to-damage ratio. It's during the sequential execution of two or three minimal techniques together that speed can be seen as a casualty: to understand this one needs only compare the efficiency of application between three moves practiced separately, and then compare them to the same three moves practiced as one maneuver. The constant practice of the moves in a group creates a gain in application speed that will outstrip the efficiency of the three moves separately.

As techniques are impulsively joined by the dictates of the moment, lengthened out to meet the demands of a situation, as fast as they are they're simply not as fast as something that has been long practiced cohesively. For this reason it's best to know which maneuvers benefit the most from something longer than one-move construction and those that don't, and practice each in what has been determined the most beneficial form.

As already said, the needs of a combat situation will determine the maneuver being organized to answer the demand, and when dealing with certain situations it's not uncommon to identify outcomes that are not only possible, but ones that are highly likely: a certain throw that nearly always places you on top for example, or a guard against a punch that always leaves an opening in the other's defenses. This forecasting of position or action wouldn't be worth attempting if the number of responses the opponent could make was too numerous, but the fact is that most people have no combat education whatsoever, and what the martial artist most times will be dealing with is not another martial artist, but rather one of the majority who are without the skill or experience that is here being discussed. The martial commandment we are living by then is 'prepare for the most probable attackers first, then everything else in order of expectancy.' That being the case, we are going to severely limit the attacker's reactions once we grapple onto him, and the lack of options that he has will change the equation in our favor. While the attacker is being clinched there are only so many places he can go and moves he can try - and we know this. A part of this truth regarding the way someone reacts in a certain situation to a certain technique is related to natural instincts, like the way we blink when someone makes a quick flicking motion toward our eyes. Try to pull someone forward and they naturally pull backwards, try to sweep them right and they pull left, grab onto them and they grab back. While they're not exactly autonomous reactions, meaning dependably reflexive and unconscious, we can still safely count on the likelihood of those reactions as a reply to the moves we intend to make. This new knowledge will assist us greatly in our design efforts. If we know which way the enemy is inclined to move when we go in a certain direction with our attack, it makes it that much easier for us to plot our solution.

This which has been discussed above, the enemy's likely reactions and inclinations, I must remind the reader is yet another over simplification, done purposely for the need to keep things brief. This automatic reaction we're using as a 'constant factor' would in truth be grouped with whatever number of other likely reactions the theoretical opponent could make, and then each of those reactions would be planned for. This will be depicted in map-form, or as a visual chart, in the section ahead concerning variable techniques, as will other material, especially as the need for visual reference becomes more pertinent.

Minimal Techniques

As stated in the preface, there is no exact definition for the terms minimal, standardized, chain or variable in the way they are going to be employed here to describe particular concepts. To my knowledge they are not standard martial nomenclature, nor have they been encountered in anyway similar to that which like they are about to be used. The loose definitions they have been assigned in this text are for the sake of convenience. This is nothing so pretentious as an attempt to concoct new terminology, but simply a means to adopt terms to satisfy the need to categorize and assess the material before us.

A technique that is minimal is one we'll define as having a small number of components, simplified and succinct. In most cases it'll be a single move, at most two. Any combination of guards or strikes or locks or throws or displacements that are completed simultaneously or in a tight series of movements – requiring only the smallest amount of time to execute – should be admissible to the minimal category. The salient traits of these techniques are their speed of application (due to their length being kept purposely short), and thus a broad applicability. This wide usage stems from the fact that these minimal techniques are often the result of basic components, like the guards and strikes and holds mentioned above. They are usable in a solitary way without the larger aim of those longer maneuvers that are applied with an expectation of high and decisive injury to the assailant.

An example of this would be an *Inside Guard* that is most often used for deflecting incoming strikes to the upper body. Dozens of longer maneuvers will make use of this deflection principle throughout the system, but due to how this deflection works it can be applied in any place where imagination and practicality support. In many ways it could be likened to fighting with the components and techniques before they were crafted into strings of components and complex techniques – meaning that the student is never limited by the lack of components, tools and concepts to create their own maneuvers if the situation demands. And given that these principles, these minimal component maneuvers, will form the greater and more complicated maneuvers later in the discipline, like those described ahead in the sections on chain and variable techniques, the learning of the latter is sped up considerably by the mastery of the former.

The maneuvers in the entry-level ranks, especially white and yellow in this particular mode of Jūjutsu, tend to be of the minimal type, as quickly learned as they are applied (keeping in mind that learned and *mastered* are two different things). This is not to imply that minimal type maneuvers disappear after the lower ranks. Even at *Shodan* (black belt) and those ranks which precede it there are minimal techniques as well as longer four- and five-move maneuvers. The minimal type maneuvers from the early ranks remain in continuous use throughout the system as they are foundational, and form the base of the system's architecture, like most martial arts.

In the absolute and uttermost minimal form, what would be considered a single-move maneuver could be comprised of only one component. If we try to think in terms that represent the greatest potential speed for application, then naturally the less parts a process has, the shorter or faster the process should be. This can be demonstrated by numerous examples, the first already stated earlier: the need to defend ourselves against one right-hand punch could be accomplished by nothing more than one subtle displacement that takes us out of line with the incoming attack (no different than a boxer's bob and weave), completing a purely defensive maneuver. An unavoidable engagement, where a preemptive strike is favorable, would make that first solitary punch that we ourselves execute against a would-be attacker a single-component technique, nothing being utilized outside the strike itself. A gunman standing in close proximity holding a small arm, any handgun, would require but one shock-strike to the offender's arm to both break his hold on the weapon and send it out of his hand. This is a list that could be expounded on for a considerable length of time given the multitude of combat principles that can be applied singularly.

The advantages of the minimal type maneuvers are clear: they promote ease of learning and speed of application, an appreciation of basic attack and defense, preparation for more difficult maneuvers and a high degree of applicability; but there are still disadvantages, and while smaller, are still nonetheless present and must be accounted for.

The first disadvantage to minimal techniques is that when they're utilized by newer students the maneuver (and skill level) is usually still in an isolated and elementary state, without the support of other skill sets or tools, and as such lacks the kind of decisive effect done by more matured solutions. These same minimal techniques become much more fleshed out in later ranks, working harmonically with other components and thus are much more impactive, taking on a more standardized length. Any technique practice will promote a skill-development in direct correlation to that practice's complexity and length (or lack thereof), and so to focus on techniques of a shorter and more conservative length is to develop a coordination proportionate to the length and complexity of the material being practiced – lesser than the coordination that belongs to the longer maneuvers of the later stages.

To experienced veterans of the art the usage of these small one-moves is a powerful tool of improvisation to supplement an already deep pool of resources. However once a martial art has a certain over-abundance of techniques in its arsenal, the greater the chances become that less and less will see usage. There will be but so many that are in constant demand, others only half as much, and some only little. This has been a pervasive truth in this writer's experience, especially if one practices more than one system of fight. A natural gravity to particular moves will incline the martial artist to use those first and foremost and others in a priority that befits their standing in the mind. It is impossible to speculate as to that number of maneuvers that represents the ideal quantity of material, or just as importantly when we've exceeded it, surpassing what was utilizable and reaching down to less accessible depths. Every martial artist would answer the question differently, some outright refusing to believe there was a depth that would defy usability - but nevertheless, the more that attention has to be spread out across a larger number, the thinner it becomes.

To assist the reader in making sense of this minimal-chain-variable maze of techniques that has been used here, a pictorial map of the maneuvers being used will be a reference point and something that the reader can refer back to at any given time to orientate themselves. Like an actual map, and at each contingency, the reader will be able to compare each newly proposed course of action with the techniques that are about to be deviated from. This type of chart, that which is directly below, will allow for a clarity otherwise difficult to attain.

Fig 6.2

Fig 6.1

Fig 7.0 Fig 7.1 Fig 7.2

Fig 6.0

Fig 5.0 Fig 5.1 Fig 5.2 Fig 5.3 Fig 5.4 Fig 5.5 Fig 5.6 Fig 5.7 Fig 5.8 Fig 5.9

Fig 8.0

Fig 8.1

Fig 8.2

In the first two images that follow (fig 5.0 and 5.1), a technique is demonstrated in its utmost minimal form: one side displacement to perform an escape from a two handed strangle. After the first lateral movement is complete and the escape is realized, we will explore the needs for lengthening the maneuver away from the minimal type toward the chain type, and finally explore the need for modification by making the maneuver variable so that it can remain effective despite complications.

Fig 5.0 Uke begins the attack on tori using a two handed strangle around the neck from the front. The arcing line displays tori's intended arm movement, which will be reinforced by a lateral footwork in the same direction.

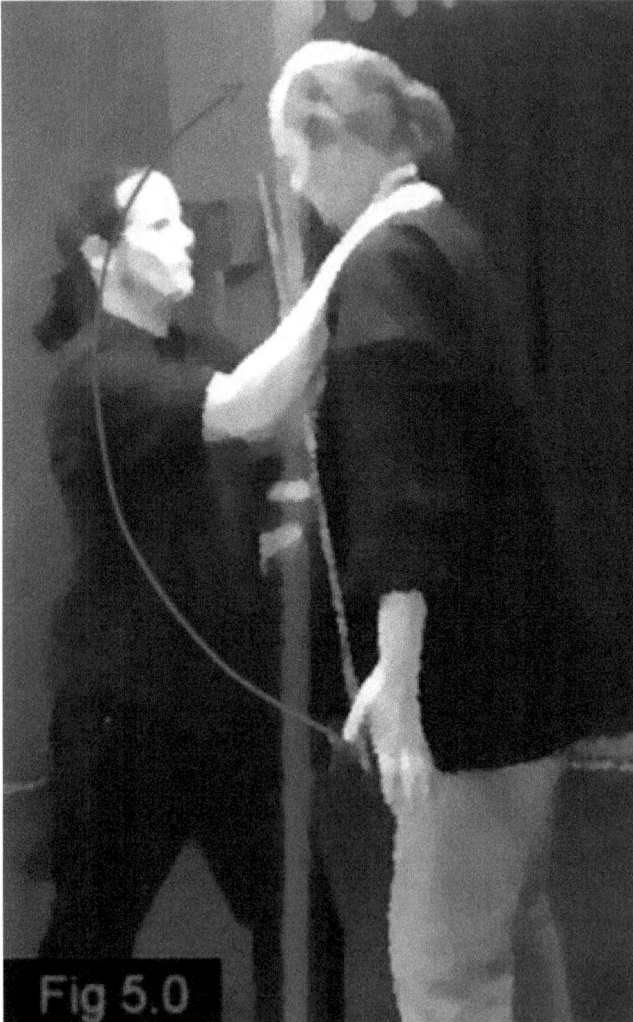

Fig 5.0

Fig 5.1 Tori performs the lateral displacement to his right, to the far side, with his left arm moving in propeller fashion across the intervening space, coming down between the two combatants.

Fig 5.1

Fig 5.2 With the displacement to the side now complete, the motion having lent enough force to tori's left arm, the strangle is broken and escape is possible.

Fig 5.2

Let us assume, however, that though the strangle is broken the escape still can't be accomplished and that the attacker has latched on to the shirt (*gi*, or uniform, in this case) and has created a clinch point at the collar with one or both hands. Here the arrow makes plain the path of the elbow strike which tori prepares to use.

Fig 5.3 shows us tori's next moves in light of uke's unbroken clinch. With ideal position, tori attacks uke with a reverse elbow strike to the head.

Fig 5.3

Fig 5.4 follows it with a complementary round elbow which receives a contribution of force from the reverse elbow that preceded it. Uke has relinquished one clinch point and is now left with only one, that being his left hand. If we allowed for clean and solid connections on both our elbow strikes, it wouldn't be so unsafe to presume that disengagement and escape are now possible (an arrow at the bottom outlining the proposed trajectory of tori's right leg also threatens a knee strike that continues to build on the harmony of elements already established and moving in the direction toward uke).

Fig 5.4

This technique is quickly graduating from something of minimal substance to a maneuver of more standard length, which is to say roughly three moves or a little more. Again the term standard, like the terms minimal, chain and variable, is not common martial terminology, and used here (and loosely defined here) for convenience's sake.

A technique having successive moves within it, applied one after the other, can obviously possess more than two, three or even four combat principles. To continue on in that direction of thought, however, creating, or maybe just trying to apply, techniques of excruciating length will often result in excruciating frustration. The greater the length and complexity of any given maneuver, the greater the need is that none of its many moves fail anywhere during application: the more components it has, the more the likelihood that one will flop. The flop may not mean that the particular move that failed was substandard, but perhaps only that it was in the wrong technique and trying to address the wrong kind of attack, or it was in the right technique but in the wrong order of movement – say move three, when it should have been move two.

Chain Techniques

A chain technique uses a long series of moves, longer than what's commonly found, and these are always in the same order. This has firstly the advantage of being able to achieve more damage in a shorter span of time than compared to the same number of similar techniques improvised one after the other. This is due to reflexive speed. As said, a chain of specific moves practiced together in order are going to enjoy a far faster rate of execution than those same moves improvised spur of the moment – no different than any technique that's reacting at reflex speed compared to one that isn't. Each component move will have reflex speed, certainly, but not the same rate of execution that they would've had if chained together in a string. It would've had to have been practiced and hammered into muscle memory as a series of actions, a chain, to profit from the kind of speed gain we're discussing now. Its grandness will be the use of that execution speed in a lengthy array of movements, which will appear as a blitz, and the resultant damage inflicted on the target at one time. The potential injury to the foe here isn't only the result of attacks that are excessive, but more accurately, attacks that are successive. One of the signature characteristics of the martial arts is the ability to attack in rapid sequence, moving from target to target. Every assault in such a barrage is built upon an opening provided by the one that preceded it, and in turn will create an opening for the one to come after it. Such a sequential method of attack makes it possible for the martial artist to bring a dizzying array of moves to bear on one offender, mounting an accumulation of injury that is often final. Good combat science, regardless of the martial art being practiced, attempts to make best use of this systematic effect, whether it be a short, minimal technique or one of more standardized length, multiple moves long. Chain-type maneuvers make more use, and often better examples, of this than any other type of technique given that the aim to inflict unsustainable damage in one single exertion requires a combination of movements uncommonly long to meet such a goal.

In a combative engagement it is infinitely more preferable to do a little too much damage than not quite enough – the former is to win, the latter is to not. We have to assume that the stakes are life itself – and perhaps not even our own life, but that of a loved one. This means that there is no room for error. When attempting to carry out any technique, the pressure to achieve a smooth execution is present, but in a chain maneuver is particularly compounded by the maneuver's complexity due to length. Any disruption to any part of its sequence will cause the maneuver to run amok, forcing the martial artist to have to abandon it in mid-execution and move to something new. An advantage, however, of chain techniques, other than speed and potential damage output, is the level of development for coordination and reflexive memory that it promotes through repetitive practice, much more than what would be gained in maneuvers of shorter length due to less substance. These chains can often be at lengths of six or seven moves, and at their very outermost extreme can exceed ten or more. While something ten moves long will undoubtedly improve muscle memory and coordination in a capacity beyond the normally expected, the unwieldy length leaves the maneuver outside what's practicable – a thing whose over-ambitious design creates a complexity that gets in its own way, rendering it not easily usable.

Nor are over-long chain maneuvers efficient, exerting unnecessary energy for the securement of a combat objective that required something markedly less. This calibration of excessive force isn't only wasteful in regards of energy, but dangerous due to the possible use of over-force – the objective will almost always be to incapacitate, but not to inadvertently murder. And a technique in excess of ten moves is positioned to accomplish severe, and potentially lethal, results. There could certainly exist circumstances that demand such lethality, but in this writer's experience the chain techniques in question were positioned too early in the curriculum and didn't address any attack that could justify such a determined and loaded reprisal, prompting the question as to why such material was being imparted so early in the system and for inadequate reasons.

Like the *chain* model's advantages, the disadvantages are unfortunately persistent and not dismissible: the *chain*-type construction is where the advantages lay; it's also where the disadvantages lay.

Remember, for the success of a maneuver that has so many moves, it becomes crucial that no one move anywhere in the chain fail, because to do so is to create disruption for everything that comes thereafter. Complications become dangerous to the martial artist because of the assumption that the opponent will be in a specific position for every move in the chain, and that he'll be in a specific condition as regards to damage already accomplished by our attack. If, for any reason, the opponent isn't where he ought to be, or not in the damaged condition we'd thought he should be, the unfolding of the chain can become snagged and jammed. It cannot ever be forgotten that this execution of moves is happening frightfully fast, and that means it cannot stop and compensate for anything unexpected.

What does this mean for practicality? It means that if the chain technique begins with a right hand strike to the head, then a round kick to the solar plexus and then the attacker *doesn't* fall like he's supposed to, and charges into us, then moves *three, four, five* and *six* never happen, and the counter maneuver the martial artist uses next is to address the tackle that interrupted the last counter maneuver. The argument that the chain technique managed to strike the offender twice in our above example, and did so due to the speed it achieves from being practiced in a fixed form, does nothing to assuage the fact that more than half the technique was inapplicable. The chances of carrying out each link in the chain get smaller as we add more links to the chain, which means the longer it gets the more unreliable it becomes. Whatever moves are at the end of the chain, irrespective of how fast they can be applied, are meaningless if they are inaccessible. Our focus here is not in the hypothetical technique above, but the likelihood of inapplicability: the average two-move technique might have a better than fair chance of success due to its shortness, but a six-move technique's chances? Ten-moves? Some are even longer. Ultimately the martial artist is left with one consideration: how valuable is the maneuver on the field when compared to the energy and time invested in its acquisition?

Practically speaking, the best chance then to bring a chain technique's advantages to fully bear on our foe is for the very first move to be executed with optimum success. This makes it clear that the application must be resoundingly optimal. The very closest we can come to any guarantee on achieving an optimum execution of any technique is if the opponent doesn't do anything, nothing whatsoever, to complicate our efforts.

Is this even possible? Yes. But the possibility is highly conditional. And just because it's possible doesn't mean it's easy or likely. It would mean beginning the attack while our opponent has no defenses up, nothing whatsoever: which means we've achieved complete surprise. Surprise is about the only state that could provide the kind of conditions needed to execute a long chain technique in its entirety. Surprise implies defenselessness on the part of the person experiencing it. We are assuming of course that the person executing the technique has an admirable mastery over it and can repeat it perfectly at will. A long chain technique, to be fully effective then, is largely dependent on an opening move that produces psychological shock and numbness. It would be necessary to maintain that numbness throughout our attack until it was clear to us that the opponent was sufficiently hurt and so unable to raise any effective defenses. The identical problem plagues the cumulative damage advantage as well. The damage cannot accumulate in our favor if the moves never have a chance to accumulate themselves – the damage ends wherever the chain broke. While the benefit of heightened coordination from the practice of long chain maneuvers is real regardless of combat effectiveness, it's simply too small a benefit in itself to justify the time and energy investiture for a performance so precarious, especially when the person may be trusting their life to it.

Plotting a reliable set of reactions for the opponent in answer to any one move we make is hard, even when that one move is something that forces the other person into a highly static and immobile position – like a clinch. In a clinch the other person has precious few moves to make, though our task of predicting their reactions is still laborious, more time-consuming however, than difficult. And after all the available moves and reactions the foe can make have been calculated and assessed, and then the countermoves approved, the martial artist still must conduct the hours of testing needed to confirm the new technique in a controlled environment, then on a field more demanding and less controlled. So the investment of resources is weighty when engaging in the design of such moves, far more so when in engaging in the practice of them. Comparatively speaking, a maneuver in excess of eight or nine moves leaves too broad a range of possibilities open for the opponent (even if they're unaware of it) to produce first a disruption, and then havoc, within the martial artist's precision attack. This disruption, the reader must understand, may not be the result of the enemy reacting with a minor deviation from the expected response – but perhaps they just didn't react enough. If one expects a roundhouse kick to the plexus to crumple the attacker forward, winded and doubled over, but the kick impacted the pectoral instead, then the attacker may simply be pushed backward, hurting and off kilter, but not doubled over. Disruption. Of course the experienced martial artist will simply continue attacking with a different maneuver when the initial technique is interrupted, and an onlooker (or the foe himself) may not even be able to detect the transition from the middle of one maneuver to the beginning of another one...but that makes the whole transition no less inefficient. The goal should be to reduce complications to ourselves as much as absolutely possible. *Difficult* may not be the right word to use to describe the function of a less-than-ideal chain maneuver, but it isn't wrong by much if the maneuver is poorly conceived. All then depends on using chain maneuvers that have been soundly designed and widely proven, but most importantly knowing when to use them – against what attacks and in what circumstances.

Two factors that help make a martial artist's attacks so powerful and so captivating to watch are their speed and their almost mystical knowledge of what the other person is going to do before they do it. This, for the sake of simplicity, we'll call reaction time and reaction type. The degree of speed a martial artist can move with translates into a loss of reaction time for his opponent as the other can't keep up. The detailed study of the possible positions and effects most likely to result from a martial artist's attack can only mean the opponent has very little to work with in terms of what could have been used to surprise the other. The reaction-types of the opponent have already been long plotted and prepared for.

With our eye still on the objective of understanding these techniques that use a chain design, we will purposely create complications to explore the process of resolution. We are going to return to the pictorial map from up above and to the technique we last seen. The assumption is that the attacker, or our uke, was not beaten by the heavy elbow strikes and remains an active hostile.

Fig 6.2

Fig 6.1

Fig 7.0 Fig 7.1 Fig 7.2

Fig 6.0

Fig 5.0 Fig 5.1 Fig 5.2 Fig 5.3 Fig 5.4 Fig 5.5 Fig 5.6 Fig 5.7 Fig 5.8 Fig 5.9

Fig 8.0

Fig 8.1

Fig 8.2

Fig 5.5 Tori attempts to finish the engagement, but first needs to determine the rigidity of the arm still clutching on to him and to do this launches a knee strike at uke's leg, hoping that the arm will weaken for a half-second when uke's leg is struck by tori's knee. Tori's intention is to tighten the distance and reduce the space between them.

Fig 5.5

Fig 5.6 Tori strikes with the knee and uke makes a grab for the collar with his free hand, resulting in a double collar clinch. With his left hand tori grabs uke's hand in what is now a completely new predicament and threads his leading leg between uke's (along the dotted line). Locked in a mutual clinch, uke realizes too late that tori is about to reap his leg supports out and unbalance him.

Fig 5.6

Fig 5.7 What transpires now is an inside leg reap (or *O Uchi Geri*) as the line beneath uke clearly draws the direction of tori's sweeping leg (a hook-and-pull back towards tori himself), and uke finds himself falling backwards as a simultaneous thrust of force is delivered to his torso. The line on top delineates driving force.

Fig 5.7

Fig 5.8 is simply the result of the forces, both sweeping and pushing described in the last picture, now being realized by the momentum of the motion and having resulted in uke's fall: the arrows depicting the divergent forces that created the balance breaker are the lines top and bottom, push and pull respectively.

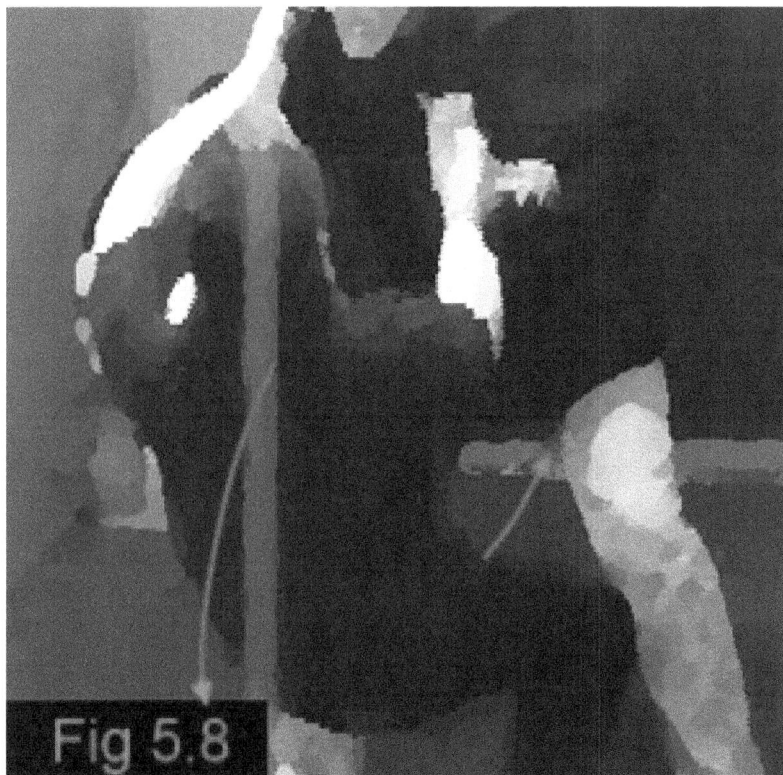

Fig 5.8

Fig 5.9 Representing one possibility of many once uke impacts the floor: tori sweeps up the end of one leg and falls back calculatedly, creating an ankle extension, and again concludes the engagement. The upward pointing arrow signifies stresses exerted against the Achilles tendon.

Fig 5.9

What Is *Jiu Jitsu*?

This six-move maneuver takes us from a double-handed strangle to an ankle extension and whose overall length constitutes a small chain technique, carefully constructed, but without any contingency support yet.

It is in our best interest then to limit both his reaction time and the ability to vary his responses. He may not have that many choices at any given stage of our attack, but that's not the problem we're struggling with: our problem is that our chain-maneuver has been built on the notion that his responses are already predetermined. If we so much as receive one variation anywhere in his reaction at any stage, the odds are that the technique will not be executed in its entirety and it'll be us, not him, who is surprised by the unexpected. The disruption of our chain maneuver by some resistance he's offered us will mean our reaction time will be delayed by surprise, leaving us to struggle to reply against whatever attack type is being used. The plan that we could stun him and so stunt his reaction time could end up unexpectedly happening to us.

For this reason maneuvers should be carefully meted out in length – number of moves as well as time to accomplish them - to allow as little reaction time and type on the enemy's behalf as possible. This in turn ensures a high success rate in application. It is impossible to apply one universally acceptable number in regards to length, or components or moves that a chain maneuver should conform to. Five may work excellently for a particular type of attack, and seven for another. Likewise it's difficult to apply a minimum number of moves to what would constitute a chain, but it seems that anything more than three moves long is drawing close to the length and dependencies a chain is characteristic of.

It's of paramount importance to recognize the value of good chain techniques in combat, and necessarily to separate them from those that are the victim of defective construction or are just simply over-thought. It isn't of the chain type construction itself that we must be wary, but of those specimens which are misguided attempts of it, in some ways not so different from techniques of minimal design that have been underdeveloped and subsequently lack enough substance to have any appreciable effect. The traits of a good chain maneuver are balanced construction and carefully conceived design – these are more than valuable, they're powerful. The dynamics that chain maneuvers use are one of the most considerable advantages to martial art training: a method that makes use of logical progression of moves during attack and defense, each move exploiting a weakness that was already there and creating a new one for the next move, so on and so forth. Done correctly they are as decisive in usage as they are captivating in aesthetics, a smooth and natural congruence of elements that exemplify the quickened devastation and genius of the martial arts.

Variable Techniques

If one uses a line of thinking that is improvisational, which is to say innovative and adaptive, and firstly imagines a particular attack, and secondly our best defense for that attack, and thirdly the possible changes in reaction from the adversary, we begin to have a blueprint for what we'd need to construct a small-scale contingency plan. As we begin this defense our opponent begins to resist and is able to complicate our efforts in three significant ways – but now knowing what forms this resistance will look like allows us to plan our maneuvers to answer each of those reactions. The original maneuver we employed will now be supplemented by three other maneuvers, closely related, but each intended for a particular reaction we know our foe is capable of making. At the end of this we should have one technique with three additions, four in total, representing a significant insight into what is meant by a variable technique.

Most martial artists respond to the changes in their attacker's reactions instinctively based on experience – sparring is excellent for developing improvisational skill – but few disciplines (none in this writer's experience) will actually bother to map out the most likely counter moves and plan for them with counter-counters with that kind of meticulous attention to detail that only recorded results and diagrams can provide. It streamlines our reactions to the opponent's reactions, reducing that greater majority of scrambling that goes on when things don't proceed according to expectations. In a maneuver of variable design, multiple techniques are brought together to be used in standby for contingencies rather than consecutively in a series. These sets of techniques, if viewed as an illustration, could be represented by a circle chart: the central and largest circle being the first technique used and the smaller circles being the fallback techniques that we may have need of. In the chart we see circles branching away from the central one that represent the complications the enemy has created (#2 and #4), and with each complication also the proposed correction we need to make (it is also a type of mapping mentioned much earlier).

The primary advantage is the preparation it provides for what might have been unexpected positions; how to easily transition from the first technique to a more appropriate one as the opponent offers different types of resistance. It gives us ready access to prompt, deft counter-reactions. The elimination of surprise is best achieved with this approach, and that is an advantage that can't be overstated. Given how the variable technique branches from one maneuver to another dependent upon need, it is expected that certain pairings or groupings will always work well together and so new maneuvers come into existence through the combination of pre-existing ones. It is actually the grouping of maneuvers that creates this unique contingency mentality, allowing for the combination of minimal, standardized and chain maneuvers for the purpose of creating variability.

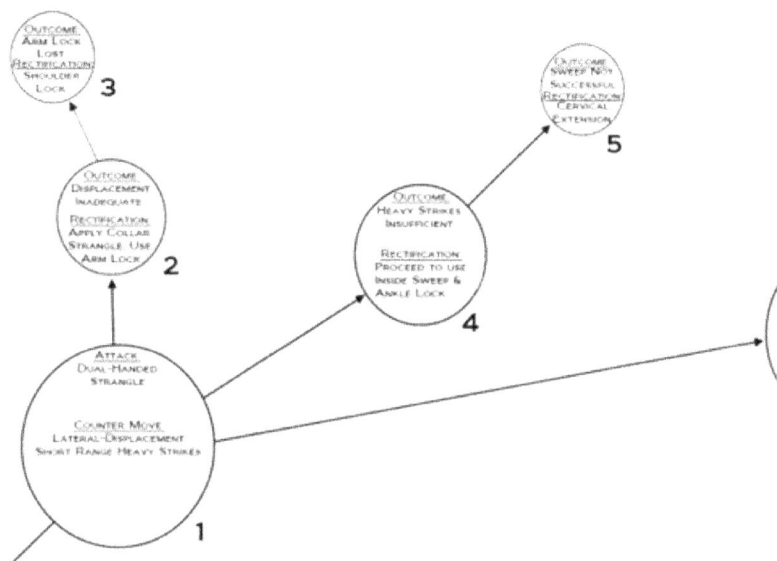

The primary drawback to variable techniques is the vexing amount of time needed to plot accurate reactions, and then furthermore the corresponding solutions (optimum groupings of maneuvers) within the martial art's architecture itself. A true variable ideal would need to permeate the entire system of fight. It would be difficult to introduce if it didn't already exist and time-consuming to map if it already did. A visual reference would almost be necessary to institute a training regimen. This is why traditional improvisational training, such as free sparring or free grappling, is usually preferred. These most definitely have their advantages and as such are quite irreplaceable, but any initiative to design and implement systematic variable techniques is not a proposition to eliminate free sparring of any kind, but rather to enhance it.

During our *minimal* technique's transition to *chain* technique, at Fig 5.5, tori used a knee strike before closing distance with uke for the leg reap, and now we will proceed as though uke resisted his attempt to close the distance and was able to keep his arm flexed and tightly clinched, quite literally keeping tori at arm's length.

Fig 6.2

Fig 6.1

Fig 7.0   Fig 7.1   Fig 7.2

Fig 6.0

Fig 5.0   Fig 5.1   Fig 5.2   Fig 5.3   Fig 5.4   Fig 5.5   Fig 5.6   Fig 5.7   Fig 5.8   Fig 5.9

Fig 8.0

Fig 8.1

Fig 8.2

Fig 6.0 represents a new direction altogether and assumes that things have not unfolded as tori had imagined. The maneuver planned to conclude the engagement is necessarily abandoned as uke escaped the inside leg reap, and a new avenue must be explored. In this alteration uke's arm remains rigid and despite the knee strike he doesn't move to clinch with his free arm, but rather prepares to strike. This complicates tori's original intentions, but a contingency maneuver can take advantage of the development: tori cranes uke's left collar across his jugular and windpipe (in the direction of the arrow), causing the other to lean away from the discomfort. However before uke can push the offending arm away and release the pressure on his neck, tori moves quickly to phase two...

Fig 6.0

Fig 6.1 is the phase two tori uses next. He pivots on his left foot, his right stepping out and across the front of uke, while forcefully twisting uke's clinching hand with the motion of his body. If one compares the halo above tori's head and the arrows that delineate the way he is moving to the smaller broken-line arrows around uke's arm, the operational mechanics can be descried: the larger pivot and step-across of tori has helped create the torquing power to twist uke's arm into the start of the bone-lock. For the security of the hold tori has clinched onto uke's clinching hand; a clinch on a clinch.

Fig 6.1

Fig 6.2 Tori's twisting motion has forced a complete rotation of uke's arm, causing uke to double over as a bone-lock forms at his elbow; the controlling force is being applied downward over the joint through the long downward arrow. Before uke can save himself his arm is fully caught within the bone lock (or *kansetsu waza*), and the engagement is now concluded, even without the consideration of the secondary wrist lock visible by the small broken-line arrow at the clinch.

Fig 6.2

A variable mentality has at its heart prudence, and prudence demands we always assume the most difficult complications will prevail: in this case that means that uke is still able to protect the arm from the impending bone lock. At Fig 6.1 we follow the arrow right to Fig 7.0 as tori attempts to use attrition tactics now, harnessing the concussive power of reverse elbow strikes, knowing his elbow lock didn't work.

Tori's elbow is brought to collide with uke's head repeatedly until either the arm being held onto softens up or the head that is being elbowed does. The reverse elbows in question would aim to impact uke's head in one of the three circles (either temple, jaw or ear), and move along that curved line in the direction of the arrow head; the dotted end of the line represents the beginning of the striking motion, while the solid line and arrow head itself represent the end of the motion.

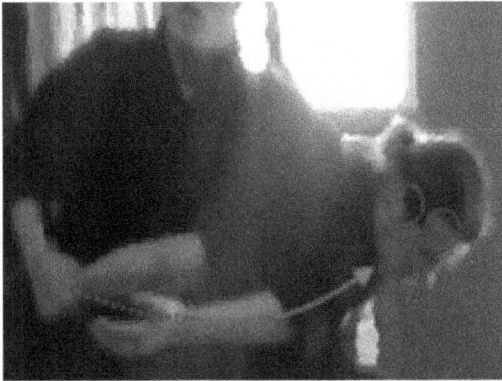

From here it appears that tori has chased the attacker's moves and reactions and forced him into a dead end, and soon all will be neatly resolved, uke having to succumb to the bone lock. Yet, for all that's been done, we'll continue to play it safe and assume the attacker has turned his head into the elbow (the forehead is one of the strongest parts of the anatomy) and is stubbornly hanging on. His arm is fully bent and flexed and so is defended well.

There will always be those predicaments where it may become a necessity to abandon the particular attack or counterattack for no other reason than because the energy being spent trying to make it function is more than what would be needed to abandon it and move on to something fresh, something unanticipated – something that will provide us with a new element of surprise instead of trying to grind some favorable result out of a course of action that's no longer vital or productive. Some such predicaments will be unavoidable, but this scenario won't be one such.

This one will work because of superb construction: clear tactical forethought anticipated this turn of events. Knowing that the situation could jam up just this way, an alternate lock called a kata waza (or shoulder lock), was introduced, executable from tori's current position.

Fig 6.2

Fig 6.1

Fig 7.0 Fig 7.1 Fig 7.2

Fig 6.0

Fig 5.0 Fig 5.1 Fig 5.2 Fig 5.3 Fig 5.4 Fig 5.5 Fig 5.6 Fig 5.7 Fig 5.8 Fig 5.9

Fig 8.0

Fig 8.1

Fig 8.2

Fig 7.0 Uke's arm hasn't locked. It is now bent at the elbow joint, nearly 90 degrees in an L-shape between bicep and forearm, and is curved about tori's waistline as seen in the dotted line. The arm is tensed and tight and not readily pliable. Tori needs but a second to feel the change, places his own left hand over the joint to confirm it and moves to a contingency plan.

Fig 7.0

Fig 7.1 Tori grasps the wrist at the end of the arm that he's been trying to joint lock, pins it to his own waist and drops his weight: tori leans his weight through his left armpit onto uke's right shoulder in the direction of the long downward arrow. The weight not only forces uke downwards, but the wrist of uke that is being pinned to tori's waist is now being pulled upwards towards tori's chest, forcing uke's shoulder to move beyond its range of motion.

Fig 7.1

Fig 7.2 Uke has fallen face first on the floor, pinned down by tori's weight and the excruciating shoulder lock that is forcing the ball and socket joint beyond its range of motion (the arrow of the curved solid line depicts the application of force). In addition to that tori is now locking the carpals of the wrist (here the force is shown by the straight and broken line whose arrowhead points downward). With a secured position above the offender, two locks complementing the position, the engagement is concluded.

Everything the reader has seen and read from the place where tori pushed the collar across uke's neck (Fig 6.0) to set up the beginning of the bone lock represents the variable mentality, introduced within a technique that was longer than minimal but still shorter than a chain. Let us now imagine again that things hadn't gone as tori expected at Fig 5.6, and when uke realized the inside leg reap was about to sweep him he repositions his leg and grabs onto tori with his free hand, creating a double collar clinch. From Fig 5.6 we follow the arrowhead south on our map to yet another variable branch that is depicted below.

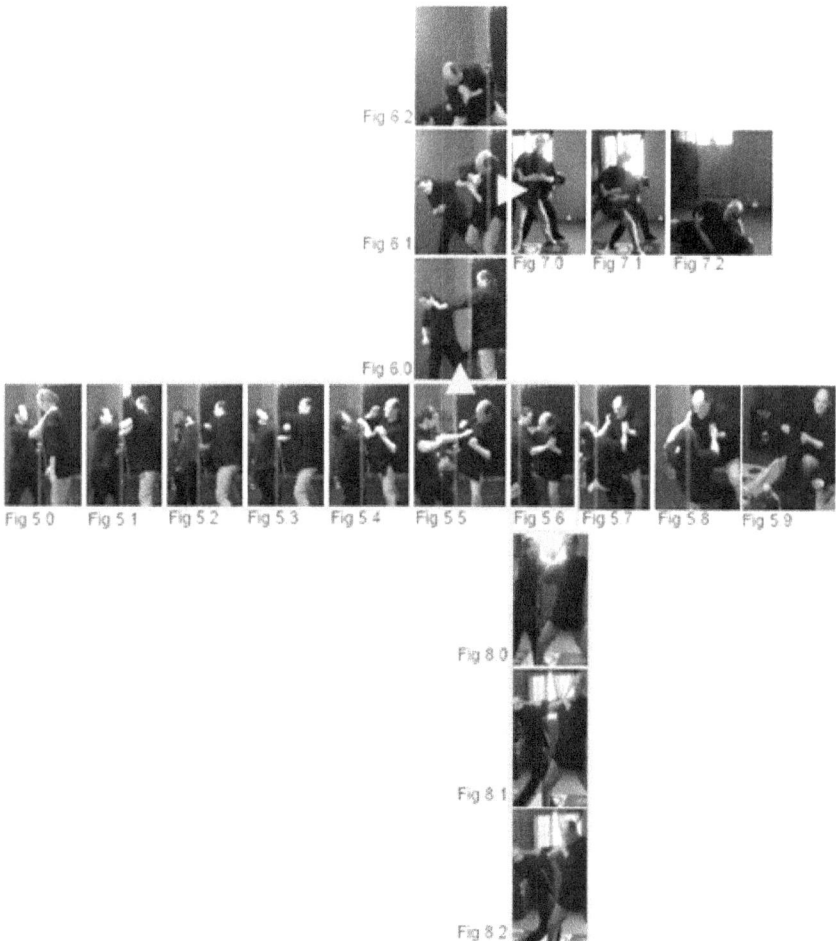

Fig 8.0 Tori realizes that the inside sweep is no longer an avenue of action. He begins a new attack on uke's head, and before the other can react the attack will be carried out with rapid execution. The arrow foretells the direction in which the force will be applied. Notice in this picture tori has bent his knees and allowed his hips to drop a little nearer to the floor, creating a kind of anchor for his center of gravity and making it more difficult for uke to move him, but also making it easier to use the force he intends to as he'll have a more stable base.

Fig 8.0

Fig 8.1 sees the quickness of the unfolding assault take effect on uke's stability as his head is craned back and his cervical vertebrae is extended, reopening the possibility of the inside leg reap again, but more importantly exposing any number of other potential attacks for tori to use. Though the arrow outlining the direction of the force is lateral here, the actual application is half way between lateral and upward; it's as the hold matures and uke falls back that it becomes lateral.

Fig 8.1

Fig 8.2 Uke's balance is nearly broken by nothing more than the cervical extension by itself. If tori chose he could topple uke here using nothing else, but still has a number of powerful options available.

Fig 8.2

This entire picture-map has provided a respectable look at what a well-conceived tactic might look like in its finished state: a minimal technique lengthened out to a small chain of moves to cope with a complication, and then the chain becomes variable, and then finally variable again to defeat the complexities.

The maneuver escalates from functioning singularly with nothing else other than its prime component – the initial displacement – to operating with close-range strike support in the form of the reverse elbows whose natural trajectory eventually include the knee strike. The most impressive trait though is its ability to use variance in its procedure and work in the direction the assailant is moving in to capitalize upon the attacker's own defenses as he attempts to complicate the counter move.

The sharpest criticism of this variable construction method is that it would need to be applied throughout an entire system's architecture to provide any immense advantage. Without this permeation its benefits are localized to the maneuvers designed to take advantage of it. It should be said that many schools and disciplines use this type of methodology, only with far more intuition, actively encouraging the improvisation approach to contingency – and while this would help make the student adaptable in the end, the result of feeling the way forward as opposed to having a predetermined way forward would mean a substantial speed reduction in usage and efficiency loss in dojo practice.

Minimal-type techniques have the advantage of being economical and concise in movement, allowing easy application to any place they are native to, without the consideration of moves coming before or after to complicate the maneuver. The downside is that they don't leverage the advantage of components that work naturally well together. For moves or components that enjoy a harmonic relationship, that complement one another too well to ignore, allowances must be made not to fail to capitalize upon three or four move combinations which will create a greater combative efficacy, speed and synergy than could otherwise have been found. This stands equally true of chain maneuvers. There are techniques of minimal construction that are just as poorly conceived as any overlong chain technique, the difference being that chain maneuvers, due to complexity, are harder to design well but repay higher. The rule of thumb regarding any type of maneuver is to discard the ineffective and attempt to replicate those characteristics that comprise everything else (and if a technique can be remedied all the better; if it can't, then it isn't kept for sake of sentimentality). With successful maneuvers – minimal, chain and standardized – sorted from all that was unsuccessful (or perhaps just not quite successful enough), it's then the amalgamation in groupings small and large to create a contingency mentality in the form of variable maneuvers and tactics, that while time-consuming in formulation, provide the best preparation once complete.

Chapter 7

Threat Assessment: Classification of Tactics

To organize the different types of attack we're likely to encounter we'll use three categories, and rank the attacks in order of the frequency with which they occur. Frequency might be one of the best ways to measure an attack's importance to us, given that the more frequent it is the more likely we'll have to fight it. If we rate the attacks using 'frequency' or likelihood, then the first type could be called *common*, the second could be called *weaponized* (for all those assaults that happen with the attacker armed), and the third could be described as *specialized* (specialized being the kind of attack that is typical of professional training such as martial arts).

Common Attacks

Our first concern must be with what is most likely to attack us, which is everything *common*. Any martial art intended for field use (although the competitive models work well in this regard also), should give the impression that a thorough assessment was conducted somewhere in their development, identifying the attacks with the greatest potential of actually happening and preparing for them. It might very well be the most paramount piece of system architecture when considered strategically. We'll use our own threat assessment here, in a categorical format, to qualify different attacks for the sake of determining their type and our need for defenses against them. While we can – and absolutely should – assess these 'common threats' to us, it is also a truth that this type of assessment, like many other topics in this book, can be applied to the martial sciences in general, even though our focus throughout will return to the system of Jūjutsu.

Neither Jūjutsu, nor any other martial art in the world today, regardless of its size (number of techniques), age, origin, lineage, specialty or overall versatility is going to excel beyond all others in every quadrant of the martial sciences. While stereotyping may not entirely work when used as a categorization tool as its assumptions are too broad and inclusive to make anything like an accurate prejudgment, lesser generalizations can certainly be applied with enough accuracy to proceed. We know that across 'system types' – whether they be of a grappling, striking or weaponized disposition – certain attributes can be universally applied and safely assumed. This is equally true for attack types. A loose and flexible rule concerning common attacks is that there won't be a tremendous degree of change in the skill with which they're applied: meaning that most people likely to use them won't have combat schooling and are relying on experiential skill only, because if they were schooled they'd be using something better than a headlock or a hair grab. If they picked up their skills through repeated fights, over and over, it's still not going to weigh in when measured against the skill sets that a combat school attendee will bring to the engagement (never mind a graduate or an instructor). Physical attributes may alter the effectiveness of attacks, common or otherwise, increasing or decreasing the effectiveness due to differences in the anatomies or natural abilities of the person actually performing the attack, but the effect will be small compared to the effect which experience will have on ability. The enhancement to attack won't be anything to the degree that the myths and lore masters maintain: extraordinary strength may allow a person to hit harder, but it won't create an extraordinary punch. Again, the common attacks will usually be just that: common. Common collar clinches, common punches, common shoves, common headlocks and so on.

For someone considering the study of martial arts it should be of some interest to know that the range of common attacks, though large, aren't so numerous that they can't be indexed and identified. The system of Jūjutsu this book focuses on uses a quite comprehensive index of counter moves to common attacks. The school the reader visits, or joins, will have their own priorities and there is no guarantee that their focus will be one thing or another. This should be investigated before committing oneself to a particular course of study. A new student, perhaps even the current reader, standing in the *dojo* (training hall) shortly after they've joined a school may find themselves wondering why certain things are taught first, and others last, and others yet seemingly not at all. This order of instruction is a direct result of the system's architecture. One answer, and usually the first and best one, is complexity. It's hard to teach someone a maneuver they don't currently possess the reflex and coordination for, nor the foundational components such as displacements, guards and comprehension of certain combat principles. The second answer is unchallenged tradition, and if this isn't questioned it's usually due to either lack of confidence or a fear of subverting the instructor's authority (for the record, it should be questioned – only in private out of respect). The last reason is related to the first: priority. The priority at the outset must be to educate the student against those attacks that are most likely to occur. And that likelihood is due to the fact that the combat principles of these common attacks are rudimentary and widely available to the greater majority: therefore these most common threats to us are threats *because* they're basic. The beginning of training has to be with what's most elementary, and with what's most expected – the two very traits that common attacks embody. The prioritization of material within the curriculum positions the student to encounter and overcome these earliest and simplest forms of violence before schooling them on the greater sophisticated forms.

Priority can't be brushed aside without disastrous effect.

Learning the defensive tactics to protect yourself from an attack like a round kick is one thing, but a fast right hand to the side of the head is far more likely as just about everyone 1) knows how; 2) currently can; and 3) already has. It is this priority, which when speaking of 'common attacks' that is created by the danger of likelihood, and that we must be concerned with. How a martial art assesses and then prioritizes threats determines what importance it places on which defenses. Also of importance to us is the quality of such defenses and where they're situated in the larger system, as this will assist us in determining where the combat's system's focus is. Common attacks are so persistent and frequent and trite that for many people – even the furthest removed from any sphere of conflict or violence – it requires next to no rummaging through memory whatsoever to find instances of them. Most acts of violence that most of us have seen can fit neatly into the common category. Leaving aside that handful of people that have experienced the extraordinary, we are left with the mundane - those that occur with a predictable regularity, but can cause very unpredictable and irregular damage.

Certain behavior, quite irrespective of culture or region, is quickly learned - like punches. Other behavior comes as so physiologically natural that it's done quite instinctively - like grabbing someone by the shoulders or collar for the sake of controlling them. Pushing is shockingly natural, probably because from childhood we see that our environment is full of natural obstacles that require the remedy of being pushed aside. It'd only present itself as common instinct to move an obstinate person who'd become an obstacle by using the same method. Hair pulling is another attack that is probably assimilated at a young age, as is the push-and-pull of any grab done for the sake of control. Not only are these common attacks, but they're boringly common, so perfectly repetitive that we eventually fail to notice them even happening (unless it's to us ourselves). We see them, experience them, as well as recognize them from childhood on – but do little or nothing to discover their remedies. And every single one could be employed with vicious effect...even conclusive effect. People often don't stop and consider the potential of a thing, especially when the thing being used is in determined hands. A hair pull can control someone and end all negotiation. Before any laughter sets in at the idea of hair pulls being serious enough to demand martial attention, think again. They are serious enough, because they control the target exceedingly well. Many Jūjutsu schools use counter-moves against hair pulls. The system of Jūjutsu being referenced here does too. The punch needn't be identified for the damage it can cause, as we all are aware of blunt force traumas and how easily they can decide the outcome of an engagement. The grappling arts have made thunderous statements about the danger of being grabbed and then subsequently pushed-and-pulled into a vulnerable position. So what was common can quickly degenerate into something far worse and all because the initial tactic – the push, the punch, the grab, the hair pull – wasn't taken seriously.

Students of combat disciplines must take all attacks seriously.

Aside from the punch, the archetypical closed-fist attack, the slap or open-handed strike to the side of the face, though not especially injurious, is perhaps even more common. One of the attacks that this particular system of Jūjutsu takes careful notice and recognition of is the collar clinch, particularly the aggressive gripping of the lapel that allows the attacker to ball the fabric into their fists for control. From the lower body the groin kick is easily the most expected, and the knee isn't far behind it, usually sharing a common target. Nor are these common attacks limited to having minimal elements, like a single punch, or single knee strike to the groin, or a forward hair clinch, but can like anything else work as two-component attacks that represent a little more complexity than that just listed.

Perhaps the most basic common attack would be the ever-typical right hand swing, as basic an attack as there is and one that populates the whole of the world – modern, developing and third – from the street corner to the bar room.

In Fig 9.0 below uke prepares to attack tori with a typical right hand punch. Tori will reply with something more specialized.

Fig 9.0

In Fig 9.1 Tori has executed a simultaneous defense and attack: with an inside guard he's deflected uke's punch which was easily telegraphed (or foreseen), and with the other hand used a chop (or *shuto*) to strike the jugular of uke at the same time.

Fig 9.1

This represents an early technique for students of more traditional Jūjutsu, one whose mechanics are easily learned, imparting good displacement principles used in tandem with upper body coordination. Any skilled puncher reading this may be objecting at the likelihood of being able to deflect or check an incoming punch, given how fast a jab can move, but they need remember that most people aren't skilled strikers; a skilled striker is a predicament requiring an altogether different remedy.

Commonly expected grapples are the headlock, or an example of a two-component grapple-attack would be the headlock-and-punch. These are but a handful of commonly understood techniques, neither bad nor good in quality of effectiveness, and for the most part usually far less than expert in quality of application, but ones that are in current circulation because they are some of the most understood and instinctive expressions of violence.

It would be a benefit of incalculable value to know the complete extent of what falls into the common attack category, because it tells us which attacks are most likely to be used against us at any given time. Consider that you might have a round kick thrown at your head or someone try to stab you or break your arm. The math is against all of those things but that doesn't mean that they can't or won't happen, only that they're not as likely to happen as a punch to the head, a kick to the groin or a headlock. What is likely to transpire is termed here as a 'common attack' and these assaults are easily utilized by the martially unschooled.

This idea of prioritization is almost of singular importance when considering the way a martial art behaves in different environments and reacts to different threats – and that should be of greatest importance to us. What we are looking for as prospective students needs to be clear in our minds, and we need to know how to identify what we want – failure to do this may result in a long investment of study with a school that isn't ultimately serving our needs or interests. There are, however, other considerations that mustn't be pushed aside under any circumstance: the first one determines the likelihood of a particular attack, and the second the lethality. Complicating this prioritization rule, however, is the idea that deadly attacks could happen with frequency in certain parts of globe, meaning simply that though we don't ever relegate them to the category of common due to their lack of frequency, a place where they occur regularly combines commonality and lethality – and this represents one of the most dire predicaments we could have to contend with. Any such place, where lethal attacks transpire with predictability, would require us to have proven and viable answers equal to the potential attack we'd be up against. This creates a new and very pressing priority, one that may not eclipse all our other needs for a martial education, but would mean that a serious focus would have to be put on a discipline that has weapon techniques in a centralized role, and subsequently anti-weapon maneuvers.

Similarly, if a woman feels her chances of encountering a situation where her sexual sovereignty may be in possible danger of violation, her combat education must favor systems of fight that address rapid resolution maneuvers, escape tactics, improvised weaponry and, lastly, ground fighting – because that's probably (though not absolutely) where the attempted rape will happen if all other attempts at escape or victory fail. A struggle will no doubt precede the ground grapple where combative control could end the engagement early. These questions should pose themselves before the reader's mind in natural response to individual needs. And the only real way to answer those questions we have is to understand how a combat system's techniques have been arrayed for instruction (architecturally speaking), and furthermore which combat problems they're best poised to answer.

The unschooled aren't efficient. They attack, like all of us, using what they're comfortable and confident with – which usually means that it's something most of us have encountered and not anything extraordinary. An easy method of control to adopt over another person is the clinch to the back of the shirt or jacket. It's not difficult and it's not visible as it approaches from the blindside...and if you've never been taught defenses against it, it's not easily neutralized – never mind reversed. This has some interest to women, given that attempts to sexually violate can happen with this type of tactile control and from this position.

In the photo set that follows we see an excellent example of a common attack, the rear collar clinch. The attacker blindsides the defender and creates a clinch on the back of the collar before the latter has any chance of stopping it. This is one of the classic control techniques a rapist might employ to violate a victim.

Fig 10.0 Uke attacks tori from behind, creating a clinch on the back of tori's collar.

Fig 10.0

Fig 10.1 As he feels the clinch tori steps wide and side on, dropping his center of gravity by lowering his hips, becoming harder to move.

Fig 10.1

Fig 10.2 Without ever stopping the smooth continuity of motion, tori takes his right arm, that which is now nearest to his attacker, and threads it upward between the arms of uke (the prescribed path of the arm is here shown by the direction of the curving arrow pointing upward); at the same time tori's far hand clinches onto uke's nearest wrist.

Fig 10.2

Fig 10.3 is eventful. The threading of tori's near arm completed, he reaches that same hand back behind uke, traveling along the side of the other's head. Again, at the same time and in perfect confluence, tori's nearest leg to uke steps out and alongside uke, mirroring what the arm up above is doing.

Fig 10.3

Fig 10.4 Tori has wrapped the near arm around uke's head and pulled it in a violent half-circle toward the direction that tori is looking, which is to uke's right (moving in the direction of the arrows). Uke is helpless not to fall as tori has taken the precaution of placing his own leg in uke's way to act as an obstruction so the other cannot save his balance .

Fig 10.4

142

Fig 10.5 Uke's attack from the blindside has failed and landed him in front of tori, with the wrist that tori originally clinched onto now a convenient candidate for a wrist lock.

Fig 10.5

The reader is urged to remember that the style of Jūjutsu that is being referenced here is Japanese and of a modernized mode, meaning it's reflective of the combative needs that are being discussed, but not necessarily what would be in each and every person's best interest. Only the reader could know what they truly need. To that end the reader must determine what is the most common and dangerous threat to themselves, wherever it is that they may live. If a person lives in an average and unremarkable part of the world, in an unremarkable neighborhood under unremarkable conditions, it is more than possible that the values, opinions and conclusions found here may be of limited use to you...the problem, though, is that we usually don't have any foreknowledge of when our safe and civilized and unremarkable environment is going to betray a remarkably unsafe and uncivilized streak.

Speaking authoritatively on a subject is a reasonable expectation after you've lived it. While I appreciate the great variance of disciplines I've experienced, and schools of thought they represented, I could have saved much money, but more energy and especially time knowing how to assess what I was looking at. I did not. I was eighteen. I knew what I liked. But what you like and what you'll ultimately need aren't necessarily going to share the same face. In the end I determined it, without the kind of help or guidance this book aims to provide, and it is probably the fact that I had to sift and wade and trudge through all the unnecessary paths that I can speak from an informed position on this subject, but it'd be a lie to say that the trade-off, the time spent for the experience that was gained, was efficient or entirely desirable. Time: hopefully, this will save you some. If you move forward in your martial art study with this at the forefront of your mind, studying tactics that will best serve you in situations you expect to be in, and then everything else in due order, you'll find yourself better prepared for the field than the guy next to you following a curriculum that's perhaps never been questioned – let alone assessed.

For most people most of the time the common attacks are the first prepared for. For many disciplines the instruction in the defense of common attack begins the development of certain skill sets that will be shaped and sharpened later. The common attacks spoken of so far are but a fraction of what's being currently used, and also should be said that even within the category of common attacks there will be those that are relatively likely and unlikely.

Weaponized Attacks

While weaponized attackers could be fought by the vast majority of martial arts (and with a better than fair chance of success I may add), they'd be best left to contend with the likes of Kobudo, Arnis, *Pencak Silat*, Kenjutsu or *Escrima* to name only some. These martial arts are weaponized by nature and each has some form of weaponry as its expertise. And it isn't only the martial arts that are focused upon weapons that possess proficiency when dealing with them: disciplines that have empty-hand combat as their central focus will almost always educate their students with disarms, and to a lesser degree to use archaic weapons. The Japanese modes of Jūjutsu will usually entail practice with the *katana* at the later stages of development, and even the *bo* (long staff) and *jo* (short staff). Practice of Karate does not usually include study of the sword, but will a host of Okinawan weapons. Ninjutsu, like Karate, has an arsenal all its own, the sword especially. Kung Fu as well will have weaponry in its curriculum. These latter disciplines whose focus is not solely on weaponry, but include it as supplement to the main program of study, will still use weaponry quite lethally – but will not be as nearly as efficient in the handling as those disciplines that focus entirely on it. Within the framework of each discipline the emphasis will differ on a breadth of goals, methodology and substance, but it is the modernized forms of Jūjutsu that will remain the focus here.

It is quite easy to stray beyond the bounds of the stated goal and try to quantify the weaponry being used in the civilian world, the areas where it's being used, at what times and by what age groups. While data like the *types of weapons* is relevant, it simply varies too much to be practical to delve into; not only does it fluctuate with whatever part of the world the reader resides in, but whatever part of that part of the world. The east coast of the United States doesn't share identical demographical or statistical consistency with its west coast, nor would one expect a condition any different in Canada, Australia, the United Kingdom or anywhere else. What small statistical data that is presented here has only been done so to aid the reader's perspective; it is done for this benefit and little else.

The defenses against weaponized attacks are important to us for more than just the disarming of the assailant, but also for maintaining the armament of the defender. From the perspective of having to face the weapon it's important to know its abilities and limitations, as much to minimize its effectiveness when used against us and also to disarm our foe of it. From the perspective of having to rely upon the weapon, caught up in a life-and-death struggle, it's important to know how to use it to best effect in our own defense, maximizing its ability, and how to protect it from being disarmed. The reader can see the relevance of understanding the weapons in question when it is we ourselves that may have to rely on it for protection. It's hard to resign oneself to the notion that loved ones, bystanders, property and our very own lives could stand or fall by the ability to wield a two foot aluminum pole. A weapon education, quite regardless of weapon type, would allow the martial artist in a desperate situation to substitute an object of similar shape and weight to stand in the weapon's stead. The importance of just how practical an understanding of weapon types are, and not only blunt force weaponry alone, is revealed in this line of thought, not only for its ability to protect us from it, but as well as the ability to protect us through recruiting it.

Many martial arts will have disarming tactics set aside for situations of close proximity to someone armed with clubs, knives or guns – and that in itself isn't so surprising given that a martial artist is one who has made themselves an expert in anatomy, as a weapon and as a target. Any synthetic enhancement, such as a hand held weapon, is dependent on the attacker's grip, as is his ability to use it. If a weapon needs to be held to be actuated and brought to bear, and the human hand is responsible for that, then it most certainly can be attacked. There exist disarm maneuvers that react to the armed hand, bat, knife and gun alike, with a congruency of speed and precision so alarmingly acute that the disarm seems unavoidable.

Even a brief examination of weaponized attacks is still a long enough venture to require something more than the space which has been allotted in this chapter, yet the goal here however will be but to outline the more prevalent weapon types and attacks, as well as the counter-mentality in the category. The use of weaponry, despite whether it be elementary or modern, is bound to be less frequent than attacks found in the common category: there is nothing more extraordinary in this than any weapon's general lack of availability as compared to the ever-accessible limbs we're born with. Violent crime statistical data for 2009 in the U.S. provides numbers indicating that less than one in every four assaults were armed.[11]

And if one looks at the years from 2003 to 2012 and the number of law enforcement officers assaulted every year, the data attests to a parallel symmetry: again less than one in four assaults were armed, in most cases one in five.[12]

What do all these numbers ultimately mean then?

To an aspiring martial artist, or anyone with an interest in such truths, it means that common unarmed attacks will in all likelihood happen more often, but that weapon attacks happen more than often enough for anyone to safely ignore. It ultimately translates into the need for a martial education that has as the nucleus of its program a formidable hand-to-hand core, anti-weapon techniques buttressing that core, and preferably complemented by weaponized maneuvers. Weaponized attacks coming in at a distant second place to common unarmed attacks tell us just how much unarmed violence is going on; not everywhere, not all of the time, but certainly somewhere, at any given time.

It's worthwhile to note that the use of weapons on behalf of the offender generally indicates a certain desperation and daring that isn't nearly so apparent in an unarmed attack. For the recipient of the armed attack it matters not at all whether the assailant's act of donning a weapon is an empty threat or not – the target of such behavior, the potential victim, must assume the threat is genuine. Failure to do this, to recognize and act upon this truth, could cause an outcome that had been a potential fatality into a probable fatality. No different than any unarmed threat, whether the assailant be a street-corner bully or an enraged motorist, the assumption must and forever be that we're in real danger. This mental posturing, always assuming the worst, is the first and best active move we can make in the position of defender: it ensures our defenses are entirely up – the attacker is denied any benefit to be gained from shock and panic – denied any advantage through catching us by surprise.

What sets weaponized attacks apart from everything else in the threat classification is the spike they represent in the level of danger. It's a leap upward that can exceed many hundreds of percent in destructive ability. A hook punch to the side of the head could conceivably knock a person out, even if thrown by a novice...but that same fist wrapped around a crow bar in reverse grip? It is the same person attacking, but they are now holding something better than a fist to bludgeon with. The difference may as well be planets apart. Though a weapon of any kind is an artificial modification to the attacker, the enhanced threat doesn't really require any serious increase in skill level to function – all is needed is the determination to use it. For a weapon to attain deadliness it requires only a hand to hold it and a will to wield it.

Statistical data from the United States between the years 2007 and 2013 tells us that weaponized attackers, while fond of guns and knives, actually preferred the use of everything else. This would comprise just about everything open to the scope of the imaginative mind, the majority of which being in the form of blunt force weapons: bats, crow bars, pipes, shovels, sticks etc.[13] From this we can safely speculate that the majority of these implements are part of the blunt force category, save perhaps the odd pair of scissors. A bat can kill as fast as a knife, and weapons with its general shape and weight are a little easier to find. What it lacks in an edge (penetrative potential) it makes up for with range and power, but not without some penalty: the lack of an edge means a great deal more energy needs to be invested, and so the weapon loses a proportionate amount of efficiency. Also what cannot be ignored is that longer weapons with their center of gravity farther from the hand are harder to handle competently, slower to swing than shorter weapons, and longer to recover. These are factors that may seem less than considerable when read in text, but when in practice, observed or experienced, they become characteristics that can make or break the attack (or defense) of the person using them.

Blunt force weapons are not the most dangerous, but they are the most numerous, and that makes them worthy of our attention. Availability means an increase in likelihood that they'll be in someone's hands who means us harm before a gun might show up in the same place. Just about every combat school in this writer's experience has taught disarm maneuvers for clubs. Usually the proposed defenses are aimed at one-handed swings, which means clubs of half-size, ignoring baseball bats and the significant threat that two-handed weapons present. Many schools don't address them. One direct and clean connection of a blunt force weapon to the arm or leg will break the said limb; that same strike to the temple, jaw, jugular can not only end the fight, but the life of the person hit, if not with the impact, then certainly after their power to protect themselves has been removed or for lack of medical attention. The amount of force released in a full swing of even a single-handed stick is pause for thought, while other advantages aren't even taken into account: the weapon is absorbing the shock of the impact with nearly no transmission of that force to its handler, save perhaps some small vibration. Not so with most limbs that are used in the same way. Martial artist's bodies undergo combat conditioning in a way that the average person's doesn't. The average mugger, rapist or bully doesn't possess those advantages either, yet with the club he doesn't have to as he only needs to swing it.

Strangely, knives account for only a small percentage of the type of weaponry usually reported in the statistics which have been used.[14] Knives are the prime specimen in the modern world to facilitate bladed attack, and this isn't so unseemly given that axes, hatchets, swords, and machetes are simply not that accessible.

As said a bat can kill as fast as a knife, but requires many times more energy, is less concealable and if swung without a critical minimum of force behind it, is closer to impotent than anything else; whereas sharpened steel requires little to nil energy to cut the carotid or tibial artery, is highly concealable, fast on attack and recovery, with almost no critical minimum of force to meet: meaning that even at the closest range it can still pierce or cut. A firearm can kill faster, and from farther, than a knife. It easily dwarfs the power output thousands of times, but a knife is available anywhere and everywhere and will never exhaust its ammunition, and its silence is an innate and stealthy trait. These comparisons are important to make for the identification of each weapon's traits. Firearms will never be replaced by something so archaic as edged steel, but edged steel will never be made obsolete by virtue of its wide practicality: it's too broadly used, too available and in combat too effective to ever be absent. Soldiers, hunters, specialized police and professionals of other spheres - all of them, in most developed nations, are issued tactical knives as a last line of defense.

Knife instructors do not delay the development of respect their students need to have for steel. From the earliest introduction the power and efficacy of steel is made terribly apparent, and then imagined in hostile hands. This sets the atmospheric tone of the training.

When you watch a certified knife instructor attack an inanimate target with a six inch blade, slice it for a depth of an inch, then explain that the material just cut is tougher than skin, denser than muscle, the weapon begins to command the deference it deserves. It can kill with one cut. Knife defenses, techniques that address assaults at knife point, are populous across many schools, in Jūjutsu as well where a background in the use of steel already exists as the discipline has a rich history of working to support the Japanese sword in warfare. The system of Jūjutsu referenced here is fully expectant of knife assault, going as far to utilize knives and their tactics when the weapon is available, to disarm it when it isn't. As said the maneuvers aren't uncommon, but for a student looking for knife training exclusively, or to someone for whom knife defense was a priority, it might be expedient to find a school that teaches it exclusively, such as the Filipino martial arts.

For an amateur assailant to assault someone, possessing only that ability to thrust and cut which any person can leverage naturally, his attacks needn't have an accuracy but only a connection to be dangerous – such is the combative potency of steel. With only a finite quantity of liquid within the human anatomy carrying oxygen throughout the circuit, it can't endure any great reduction before the system undergoes catastrophic failures of function. Impalement by the knife's point is arguably worse than being sliced by its cutting edge, with such wound types having a propensity to induce internal bleeding, puncture organs or sever major arteries. Conversely, a knife as a weapon of defense in the hands of someone protecting themselves can be the reason they and their family live to tell the tale, especially if they'd taken the time to receive instruction of the weapon in a training hall. A surpassingly excellent instance of a knife's lethality and ability to turn an otherwise lost engagement around happened on Vancouver Island, British Columbia, Canada in 2002 when a man over sixty years old fought, killed and survived an attack – not from a human, but a mountain lion; an adult male cougar. The knife blade was reported to be just over three inches long.[15]

Even with a firearm as the weapon of choice, one that so clearly surpasses in power and sophistication the blunt and edged models mentioned thus far, the scenario still falls into the weaponized category. The more typical firearms – handguns, rifles and spread shots (to some degree assault rifles depending what country you're in) – represent the single most powerful category of armament that a civilian can access and use outside of that hardware exclusive to the armed forces. The power achievable through chemical reactions means that even the bullet from a smaller model of handgun such as a 9mm is capable of reaching a velocity anywhere from eleven to thirteen hundred feet per second (or more). Small arms (handguns) are popularly accepted to have a combat effective range (in terms of targeting accuracy), up to fifty yards (roughly forty-six meters or one hundred and fifty feet) and enough penetrative power to go through-and-through a human being with a full metal jacket round. Using lesser penetrative ammunition, such as hollow points, can consequently end up taking a far steeper toll on the target as a great deal of the kinetic energy is transferred from the round into the mark, the bullet left within.

With many magazine capacities for small arms providing ten-plus rounds, each fired as fast as the finger can pump the trigger, and it isn't challenging to understand the immediate empowerment a firearm represents. An operational design intended to be used at range naturally provides time to aim and discharge the weapon, reload it if necessary and all while prioritizing the threats then currently before the shooter on the field. Technically, the closer the weapon is to its target the greater the impact it'll have (power as well as accuracy) but for all that it really is more deadly at range, because if that distance were great enough it could preclude all possibility of disarmament. From laser sights to scopes, to a variation in ammunition types, to light weight one-handed usage, the firearm is not a threat that can ever be viewed or reacted to lightly.

Accessibility for the civilian varies from nation to nation, state to state, province to province and territory to territory; but for the criminally-inclined, with a little nerve and enough coin, the process of procurement is close to identical across just about every country. This effectively means that a disparity exists between the moral and immoral, lawful and unlawful concerning the acquisition of firearms: one, the moral, satisfies the conditions required by due process; the other does not. This lopsided accessibility to the weapon contributes considerably to our dilemma. Depending on one's country of residence a firearm can be anything from easy to hard to impossible to acquire for the honest citizen, but with equal concern for those persons who can acquire the weapon as much as for those who can't, the understanding of the unarmed martial considerations surrounding a firearm – its use, fallibleness, advantages – are immeasurably valuable.

A healthy number of combat disciplines possess maneuvers and tactics for hypothetical confrontation with an attacker armed with a gun. It is obviously the first choice for armament, but there are characteristics of its usage that are crucial to comprehend for a person assessing the need to disarm an assailant of it, or on the other hand protect their own from being disarmed. Between drawing the gun, releasing the safety, aiming and discharging a round from it is the passage of time – it is this span of time, no more than half-seconds, that concerns the martial artist who is facing the firearm threat. The paramount question is whether or not enough opportunity exists for the defender to attack the assailant preemptively and neutralize him or his advantage before he can use the weapon. What is sought for in disarmament maneuvers is that essential amount of time and proximity, and to a lesser degree position, to execute this preemptive maneuver.

What Is *Jiu Jitsu*?

Considering the dangers posed by firearms, the worst case scenario is that the attacker armed with it has already drawn it and aimed it and has only to pull the trigger and fire to attack. This situation paints a picture of advanced readiness on the part of the attacker and so represents the most difficult circumstances to react to. The martial artist requires proximity above all else, more than specificity of position and more than time, because without the latter two the chances might be miserably low of success, but it's still possible to try – without proximity or closeness to the target all possibility of trying is removed. Attempting to close the distance to a firearm, even the smallest one, that is ready to fire upon us is the worst prospect in this exercise. The conundrum presented here is that the proximity needed also increases the accuracy and power, and hence lethality, of the gun trained on the defender due to having to move in the direction from which the projectile is originating. This would be unavoidable in such a scenario.

Striking disciplines, martial arts that favor blunt force attack, often have extensive programs of precision percussion, using a numerous variety of kicks and punches on tiny targets all around the student. From this base they take the gained precision striking skills and focus yet on smaller targets that are within reach, and eventually are able to consistently attack areas smaller than a human hand. Grappling disciplines such as Jūjutsu use percussion as well, but rely more on manipulation to achieve a particular outcome: locking the fingers or torquing the wrist creates a condition whereupon the hand opens involuntarily of the owner's will. The hand is highly susceptible to all these attacks, particularly the carpals, metacarpals, phalanges and flexors of the forearm. Compounding the hand's vulnerability is the habit of exposing it to attack at the end of an extended, and hence unguarded, arm. This is especially true when the hand is weaponized, usually a result of the assailant wanting to incite intimidation through the display of the implement, whether that be firearm or anything else.

It is against the appendages responsible for operating the weapon that the martial artist will focus his attack, knowing that the weapon cannot be utilized without the hand holding it – once the hand is maimed or destroyed, the threat is significantly, if not totally, negated. There exists in Japanese forms of Jūjutsu, as well as others, the maneuvers needed to disarm knives, guns and clubs from varying postures, as well as various elevations and positions to the front, sides and back of the martial artist (and in the case of clubs and knives, in various states of swing and thrust).

Fig 11.0 Uke attempts to cut downward across tori's face with a six-inch blade in a diagonal down cut, an arcing motion that follows the arrow toward tori. As uke begins to attack, tori moves to deal with the incoming weapon by deflecting it at the middle of uke's forearm, contacting and *redirecting* the motion of uke where the circle is. Tori never actually tries to stop the movement of uke's weaponized hand, but rather to guide it upon a new travel path.

Fig 11.0

Fig 11.1 With the most difficult part accomplished, the checking of the weaponized arm without receiving a cut, tori's far hand now clinches uke's wrist. This is an advanced throw, and though being utilized against a knife in the depiction below, would be inadvisable to attempt unless by a long-studied student in the discipline. The left arm of tori that performed the block guides the knife-arm of uke in much the same path the attacker was intending to use, making sure however that it moves downward and misses tori, drawing out a downward curving path that is shown in the picture. The path carries the knife-wielding arm of the uke along with the force of the redirection, and must be stated here that the technique in this description happens shockingly fast, a fact that makes it possible to guide the attacker's arm with seemingly small effort. As tori does this four directional throw (or *shiho* nage: pronounced '*shee-ho-noggy*'), his far side leg, the left, now steps across the front of uke, even as the arrow indicates, and in concerted effort with the actions of his two arms creates the position necessary to continue the power-generation needed for this dizzying redirection to succeed.

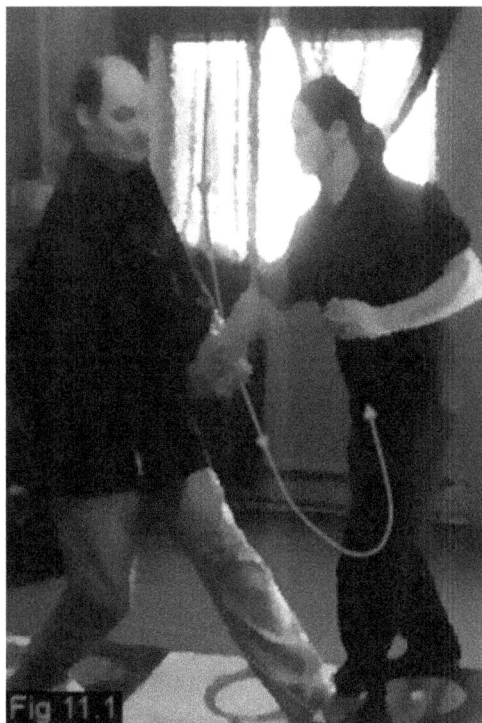

Fig 11.1

Fig 11.2 Tori's step across the front of uke is now complete, and the motion hasn't at any time or place stopped since the initial deflection of uke's knife cut began. The far side arm of tori, that which deflected the knife arm of uke, has completed a half-circle and is now clinching the wrist below the weapon, the same as tori's right hand. The halo above tori illustrates the current and continued direction of the person performing the throw, and the curvy upward arrow likewise continues to announce the travel path (again, the movement of tori here is integral to the redirection of uke's weapon hand).

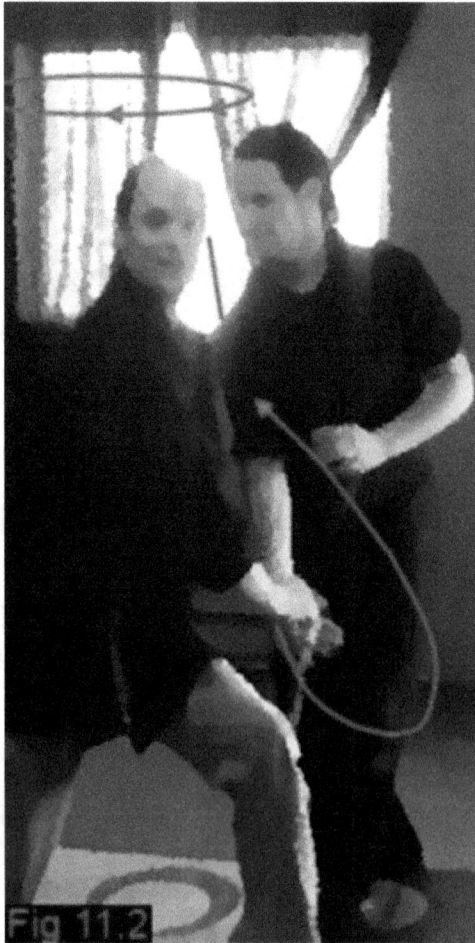

Fig 11.2

Fig 11.3 Reminiscent of the momentum-based maneuvers so favored by the philosophy of Aiki-Jūjutsu, the deflection continues in a full circle as tori pivots beneath it, the motion forcing uke's shoulder to lock and forcing him to turn as a result.

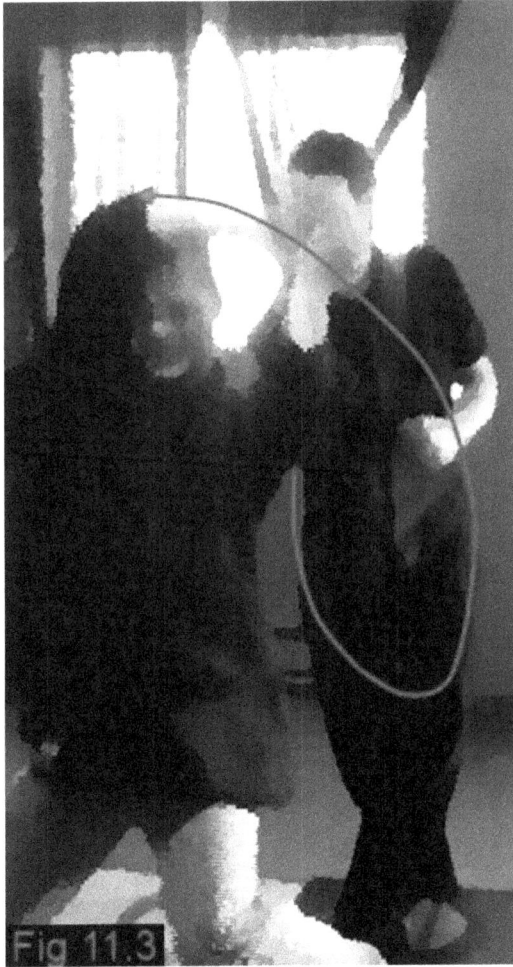

Fig 11.3

Fig 11.4 Tori has all but completed the pivoting movement needed to attack the shoulder of uke and break his balance, if not dislocate it, and the end of the motion begins to bear resemblance to a downward sword cut (the line still predicting the path that uke must follow). The reader will notice that a halo is now over uke's head as well as tori's. Each of these circular tracks serve to remind us of the way in which each person is turning, and also to make clear that each person is moving opposite to the other.

Fig 11.4

Fig 11.5 Uke, after having been forced to turn due to a progressively deepening lock of the shoulder joint, is finally pulled backward and straight to the floor with tori knelt adjacent to him, still holding the offending hand (the clinch of the hand is within the circle in the photo). The hand of uke has since been disarmed through the loosening of grip which occurred incidentally as the technique was executed. (Note: the weapon, even if held onto by uke, could also be pulled free at the end of the throw or even without the entirety of the throw itself, using the joint locking properties of the shoulder lock).

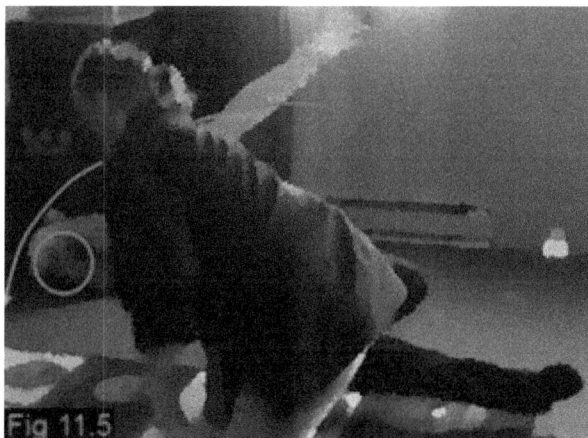

Fig 11.5

Gun neutralization maneuvers are no more complex or difficult to learn than those that attack with the goal of disarming a knife...the difference, however, lies in opportunity. The knifeman, armed with his blade, is able to throw it certainly, but unless is possessed of very special skill would be better off restraining the impulse to throw it (and waste his weapon) on what could amount to a single shot; he would be better off to hold on to it and apply it in cuts and thrusts. But in order to accomplish the latter plan of slashing and thrusting he must close the distance and come to within arm's length of his mark. Not so for the gunman. Technically he needs only line of sight, and at his own discretion can ignore distance entirely; the argument may even be made that he need not even have line of sight, but with perception and judgment, discharge his weapon through a wall to hit his mark. The ability to attack from a distance is the firearm's chief advantage and greatest complication to someone facing it unarmed. Neither of its advantages, power and ease of use, equals the benefit of being able to attack beyond its enemy's own effective range.

This is undoubtedly the most grievous limitation in our scenario: it must require less time to cross the distance between the gunman and the proposed martial artist than it does for the gunman to attack. In the end, not a deciding factor but one too large not to be central is the amount of distance that must be crossed. Three feet or a meter is one thing as the assailant is within striking distance, but anything greater and the difficulty quickly graduates into a desperate gamble. The disarmament requires proximity. In cases where the gun (or knife, or bat) is held within a few feet of the target, poised to strike, the martial artist has already practiced countering all weaponized attacks from close quarters, and done so continuously. Drawing *any* weapon in close-quarters plays to the martial artist's strengths and allows him to use all his skill sets to greatest advantage. And even without the benefit of proximity, the club and the knife can still both be addressed with longer and more paced tactics. The gun, however, if pulled and aimed at range can only be addressed by finding cover that must be sufficient enough to survive the discharge.

The hypothetical scenario in question would of course also be influenced by factors such as available traction between foot and floor, the quality and luminosity of the lighting, any distractions in the immediate vicinity, debris between the gunman and martial artist and their mutual experience in their respective skill sets: is the gunman an experienced shooter or an amateur? Is the martial artist a student or a master? Is the combat environment one of reduced space and close-quarters, or is it an open field or parking lot? A sword is a powerful edged weapon in even unskilled hands, but used inside a structure with a typical ceiling height and hallway width is relatively useless though it be in an expert's hands. The height of the person using it plus an additional three feet for the weapon itself would effectively mean it can't be used for vertical cutting, the same would be true in a hallway where it can't be used for horizontal cutting. So without the spatial dimensions necessary the sword would become a little less than a clumsy spear. A firearm is restricted in many of the same ways when in a closed and tight area with many twists, turns and cavities, all of which allow someone to come to within reaching distance of the gunman. Some walls will be too thick to shoot through even if one knew where to aim and this is a serious consideration using a weapon that has a delicately maintained stamina that is dependent on how many rounds it can hold, with no guarantee the shooter has more to feed it with.

For those who own and use firearms as the chosen means of family and home defense, the study of disarmament has a whole other benefit outside of the ability to attack someone bearing a gun, but now serves the purpose of prepping the gun owner to prevent the disarm of his own weapon. It's much to the advantage of such an individual to understand the methods by which the weapon can be knocked from the hand's grip, wrenched back toward the shooter, removed and relocated to the attacker's possession or otherwise fired while still in the hand of the owner: potentially being turned upon targets that the person applying the control-hold designates. Protecting the weapon from disarm as opposed to disarming it from a hostile, presents a significant attraction to anyone in a field of work where firearms are carried or used. It's an investiture to safeguard one's own weapon in an occupation that obviously needs it, and one where there should be no possibility that an aggressor can come into possession of it.

So, can a gunman be disarmed? Yes, believe it. Like all parts of the anatomy the human hand is susceptible to any number of attacks.

Many disciplines teach tactics for the purpose of confronting a weaponized attacker, Jūjutsu not least amongst them. Many schools do not. If this were a priority for an aspiring martial artist, then the presence of disarming tactics should be confirmed before enrolling – it should also be confirmed as to when they are taught within the system's architecture. If a person understands how a weapon can be seized and taken from them, they'll be far more effective at preventing it. A police officer for example, though no doubt trained to resist and thwart disarm attempts, would be in a far stronger position if the skill was as honed as what one might find in a serious *dojo*. To attain that caliber of skill though, like a *Shihan* (Master) of Jūjutsu might display, would require a substantial commitment to the study of that discipline. Essentially it would mean a lifestyle change to introduce the necessary training and facilitate its being made part of the student's reflex abilities.

D. S. Hopkins

Specialized Attacks

The term specialized attack is used here to denote assaults that are either highly elitist in principle of operation, complex in execution or demanding in conditioning: exactly that which a martial artist would be trained to use and attack with. A specialized attack is one being executed by an expert in hand to hand combat, and like weaponized attacks, requires immediate special attention. The number and quality of defenses a combat system has for use against specialized attacks, like those techniques that would be used by other disciplines, reveals something of the types of attacks which that combat system itself will likely be capable of. If a combat discipline can defend itself against side kicks, then it's not unreasonable to assume it may be able to utilize them.

Anything specialized is uncommonly skillful and only expectable from the minority, not the majority. Jumping-spinning heel kicks and compression locks are specialized maneuvers, as are blood chokes, eye-strikes and right crosses. In truth, the majority of people don't even know what they are let alone how to apply them. A specialized attack is just that: a specialty in assault, a combative action of higher and excellent standard, whether that excellence be founded in complexity, conditioning, operation or all three. From the perspective of each martial artist just about everything in their arsenal of attack and defense is particularized to their discipline, but specialized as far as anyone without martial art schooling is concerned, and when these persons reply to the common attacks as we've been calling them, it's with specialized maneuvers.

Within the wide realm of specialized attack the possibilities are quite vast. Kick boxers can deliver roundhouse kicks as dangerous as any baseball bat, dizzying in speed, combination and unpredictability; a Judoka can slam an opponent to the floor in more ways than most fighters can prepare for; boxers strike with a dexterity and power of hand unmatched by any other discipline; Thai fighters have shins that can break two-by-four pieces of lumber, and knees that are just as dangerous; Sambo fighters can lock a leg, break it, before the realization sets in that the leg is in serious danger; Aikidoka are renowned for redirection, and especially the myriad of ways they can lock and break any bone in the arm, hand or wrist; an expert in the discipline of *Kali* could open the ulnar or radial arteries before the hand in question could be safely put out of harm's way; serious proponents of Jūjutsu are perilous to engage in tight quarters, able to manipulate any close position.

One of the most thought-provocative possibilities of specialized attacks is that they could be brought into friction with one another, no different than the present day MMA competitions, the tournaments of old or any one discipline applied against another in a dark, unobserved corner of an unregulated world.

While the attacks and defenses of any given combat discipline could be fielded in direct opposition to another entirely distinct martial art, there are sharp considerations that immediately begin to factor in. Regardless of the impactive factors, as paramount as they are, any given combat system doesn't require anything more extraordinary than the tools it already has in its possession to close and engage with another martial art, but without at least a little forethought on the venture it wouldn't be deemed wise to thoughtlessly try it.

Without knowing what to expect on a technical level, or a tactical level, the experiment could turn out to be quite humbling – more so if our opponent is using a system of fight that has already prepared to meet the threats that our own typifies. Preparation is a decisive factor, and usually the system that has been preparing to meet a certain threat will perform noticeably better against it than it would have without the preparation. The word preparation is one layered with degrees of course. Preparing to accomplish something with a set amount of tools is one thing, combining and improvising those tools to carry out new or unorthodox functions is another level of preparation altogether – and adopting new tools from other textbooks of other martial arts and integrating them with what we already have is probably the final extreme in preparation, and the most advisable.

In the photo set that follows we see a specialized attack in the form of a power roundhouse kick applied against a specialized defense of Jūjutsu, especially built to counter the threat.

Fig 12.0 In the technique that follows uke levels a roundhouse kick at tori's ribs, an attack wherein tori accepts the power output against the bicep so that his arm can ensnare it from beneath. The travel path of the roundhouse follows the shallow curve of the arrow moving from uke to tori.

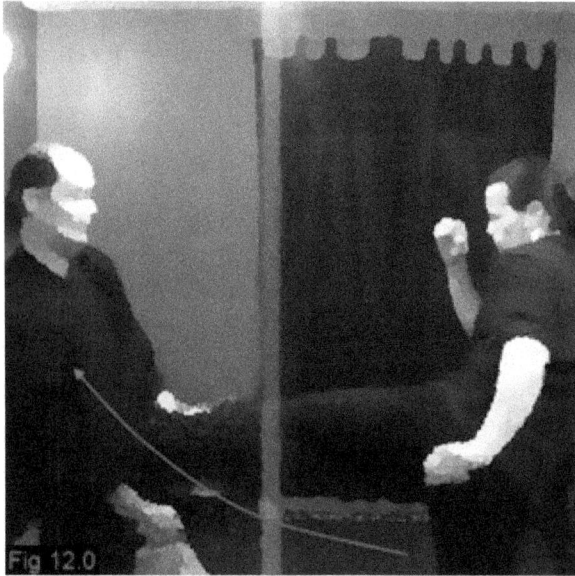

Fig 12.0

Fig 12.1 Tori takes the kick and uke, though maintaining balance, cannot retrieve the captured leg. The halo above tori indicates the direction in which he intends to pivot, while the smaller dotted circle about uke's leg indicates the direction in which tori will torque the leg – both motions are integral to the technique and work like gears, but it is the turning of tori in the direction of the halo arrows that will facilitate the generation of torquing power, without which strength alone would have to be utilized and thus the torque would be greatly diminished in power and efficiency.

Fig 12.1

Fig 12.2 Tori torques the leg over in his grip with relative ease due to the pivoting motion that is providing him power, rolling the leg of uke as though he were turning the flat of uke's foot skyward; to tori it would turn counter clockwise. As the crook of the knee (the fold behind the leg) comes into view tori drops a hammer elbow down on it to quicken the effect that the roll of the leg already has on uke: his face is gradually being forced away from tori, exposing his back.

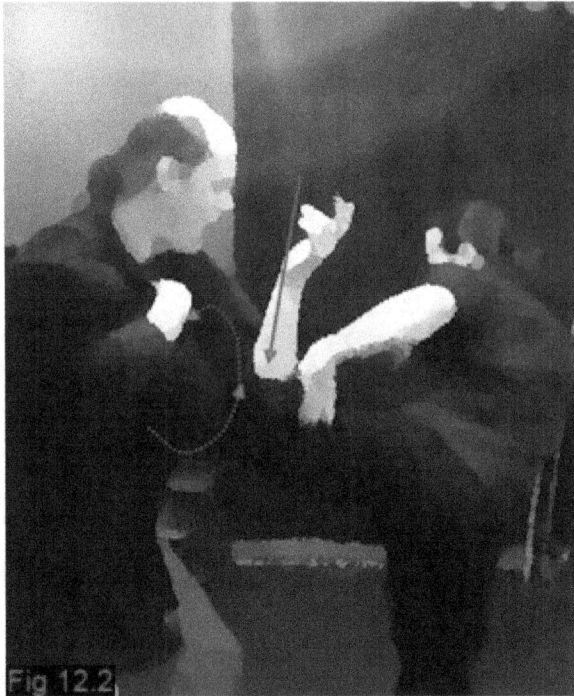

Fig 12.2

Fig 12.3 This cannot go on for long, and uke's balance has no choice but to break. He begins to fall. The roll of the leg alone was detrimental to uke's stability, but the hammer elbow and then the continued downward force (the arrowhead) of that elbow is irresistible (now a constant motivator for uke to go earthward).

Fig 12.3

Fig 12.4 Laying stomach first on the floor, uke has only half a second before tori ends the conflict, but try as he might he can't struggle against the hold on his leg fast enough to free himself, because the hold itself, though not a joint lock, precludes his rolling to either side in any significant way.

Fig 12.4

Fig 12.5 Tori here has the choice of using a compression lock (or squeeze lock), a torque of the ankle, or the mount of uke's back and the possibility of a choke – the circle indicates the nearest joint for tori to attack.

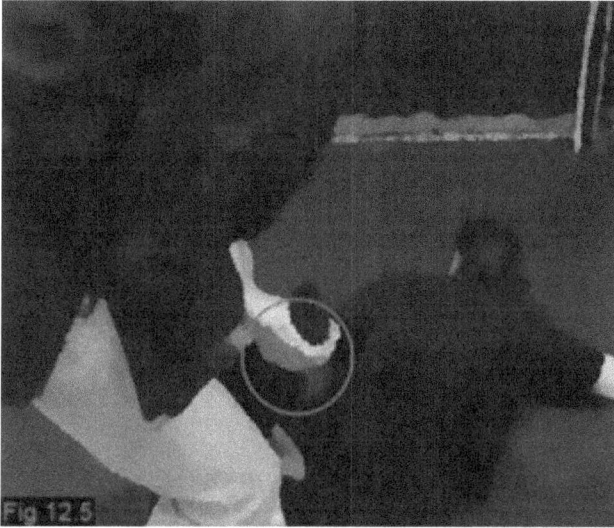

This is but one simple example of nothing more complex than a roundhouse being caught by an ensnarement. There are countless possibilities when disciplines begin to bring specialized techniques into friction with one another. No one system of fight will be able to familiarize itself with every possibility, nor adequately prepare for every eventuality – the sheer volume of specialized attacks represented by so many disciplines would be far more theoretical trouble than practical payoff. Advanced maneuvers that can counter sweeps, joint locks or unconventional striking tactics require slow and patient instruction, conditioning exercise and complex execution; the upside is that these conditioning practices and counter-maneuvers will be made up of the same components and principles of operation that exist already within a martial art, and in all likelihood won't be anything too dissimilar from them. It's not uncommon to find combat disciplines that on one hand will teach a maneuver, then a defense for it. Not everything has a counter, however. Many locks and torques and chokes and holds are irreversible by the person captured if allowed to be completely executed. Many are inescapable. And the best defenses against these are preventive: knowing what they are, how they're applied and how they work. There are defenses, preventive or otherwise, for everything, but their counters can't always lead us backwards, as through a circuit of motions, to a place where the move is simply *undone*.

Consideration for the specializations of other disciplines is the topic we must consider here. Our own maneuvers aren't truly our first concern, given that we understand them well enough to avoid them when they're in another person's hands. The specialized maneuvers we find in other disciplines is more murky terrain. From discipline to discipline, type to type, there are usually a number of techniques within them (and the principles those techniques use) for which we have no point of reference, let alone counter-maneuvers for. But as said above, it would be a pointless affair in exhaustive preparation to firstly try to imagine what those *general* needs might be – how countless – or allot the time to practically prepare. As already stated earlier, stereotyping is an action too broad and too inclusive to yield accuracy when it's applied, but the more mild generalizations can be safely made. For example if the discipline we're facing is of the grappling species, it wouldn't be sound game theory to engage them within the reaches of their expertise, even if ours is similar. Rather, it would be sounder to use what striking or weapon tactics we have at our disposal and attempt to lure them into a sphere of fight where their best strengths will not factor in yet ours remain adequate. If their system mirrors our own it'll be a chess match, individual skill against individual skill, and will not come down to maneuvers so much as it will to tactics.

What Is *Jiu Jitsu*?

Facing down a threat that is of a different species entirely, such as a breed of striking art facing down a breed of grappling art, would require the application of the generalization up above but not the stereotyping. Stereotyping as a means of categorization fails because it attempts to assign too fixed a form and ignores subtleties and minutia, which makes it a very tempting but unsafe practice. Loose and flexible generalizing may be only a little better but it allows overarching truths and rules to be assigned with relative safety, though it may not be as beneficial as stereotyping pretends to be. A general truth is that a grappling discipline of any kind will attempt to choke the distance at the first opportunity, that its weapons are close quarter qualified and that it has far fewer instruments to use at range. These truths serve the striking species well in the scenario above. Regardless of which is which, the more one knows about the other's capabilities the better the chances of survival; the effort to prepare for whatever is on the other side of the ring is after all the entire reason hybrid systems of fight emerged in MMA. The strategy of diversification worked, amalgamating skill sets from distant points of the martial compass, but it came at the cost of the deeper, more focused expertise.

The notion of a specialized attack coming into friction with another specialized attack of a different breed, or one martial artist against another, isn't as likely as one might initially think in common street violence. Most people have no hand-to-hand combat education and so it's unlikely the person you encounter in a violent altercation will have background training of any kind. In this writer's experience there were very few instances where a friend or colleague schooled in a hand-to-hand background was challenged at the street level; and when they were it wasn't by other martial artists but by persons using common-attack tools. Launching common techniques against something elite in nature, though not impossible, could be likened to trying to drown a shark or out-claw a cat, given that the counter maneuver will be specialized, actuated by an individual schooled in some form of hand-to-hand. For an aggressor to proceed with common assault tools and tactics, knowing full well they were up against something specialized, would constitute a highly haphazard act.

Chapter 8

The Power Of Methodology

Within the realm of hand-to-hand combat there is always a constant exertion of factors influencing the scales, weighing and counter-weighing. Some of these are well known, others not so. Yet knowing what they are only serves as but a beginning. What is really of interest is how much they affect the combat equation (if a term for so fixed a process can apply here).

If we examine athletics like soccer, golf or tennis and sought out those most salient factors that determined victory, it would mean analyzing each competitor's performance, which would in turn lead us to a detailed evaluation of technique – the elastico, the rotary golf swing, the volley – in an attempt to measure the skill level of the victor and then weigh it against the vanquished. Once that was done we'd have to assess how that technical usage on behalf of the winner was applied using sound tactics. In each sport – soccer, golf, tennis - the winner would consistently demonstrate an excellence of technique and tactics.

Skill is always the chief determining factor and the one constant that outweighs all other contributing factors combined. If someone unskilled enters into an engagement with someone who is, all the conditioning and natural advantage and luck in the world is worth confetti, and not a mountain of it will turn the tide in their favor, because they're simply outclassed. Naturally this isn't hard to follow: any amount of techniques that are needed to function in the athletics named above like the rotary swing, snake or backhand are integral to performing and winning. The real question we need to ask ourselves here is not what was the determining factor for victory - we know that answer can only be skill - but rather what were the smaller contributing and complicating factors that could exist outside of techniques and tactics.

If one tennis player is taller, longer limbed and more lithe than the other, does this translate into an advantage in the way of reach? At a glance it may look like a significant asset, until we ask ourselves how good the taller person's backhand is, how good their volley is, and so on. The reach in the end would only serve as much as the person possessed technique to use it with – without skill level, even the most basic, the longer reach would be nigh on worthless. If skill level between the two competitors were approximately equal the reach might suddenly have some value, but in order to ascertain that we'd have to know which moves stand to appreciably benefit from this increase in reach – only a select number would - and then by how much. The next question would be how many moves like this were made throughout the game. Following this line of questioning it starts to make clear as to how such a physical advantage is limited to a support capacity to a limited number of moves and only then with sufficient skill exists to perform those moves. What complicates the question of the value of physical advantage further are those varieties of physicality that are harder to measure in a combat environment and harder to detect in our opposition: better eyesight or hearing, more accurate or faster reflexes. These would be nowhere as apparent as weight or height or conditioning, but very well may affect the outcome more so.

The more one steps away from the picture, and so is able to see more of it and consider the process, the more obvious it becomes that factoring in things like anatomy, shape, weight, and height reduces in relevance as the level of skill increases.

If two amateur tennis players of roughly the same potential (or soccer players, swimmers, MMA competitors or anyone else) were given only a small handful of lessons at the same time, the reach or height benefit of either anatomy will in such a situation enjoy its greatest value. The reason for this is that the lack of skill level on behalf of both parties (the paltry few introductory lessons making skill as a factor nearly void) would necessitate the usage of more instinctive means to achieve what the absence of know-how could not, meaning a dilettante struggle relying more on natural advantage than specialized competency. In such a scenario, with skill sets native to the sport or discipline in question notably missing, every natural advantage is quite understandably leveraged to the utmost as the contest becomes a crude scramble for the superior position. With any technical understanding still in its infancy the emphasis of the contestant will predictably be on any tools that will provide even a small degree of control, and those tools will be those which come most naturally to reflexive control.

To appreciate the contrast between the governance of method and the absence of method, we need only contrast the difference in an attack when it is executed twice: in each instance the aim of the maneuver will be identical, but the first time will be carried out using common knowledge and tools, the second time using those specialties typical of the martial sciences. The common attack will use inefficient method and be easily recognizable, requiring no understanding of combative concepts to use. The two approaches to the same attack are nearly diametrically opposed in terms of sophistication and efficiency, the first rudimentary and ungainly, the second articulate and proficient, and this contrast will allow us to attain a certain insight. The common attack is one that just about every reader is familiar with and the damage being sought for is obvious.

Let's imagine two combatants at the outset of an altercation moving first to a clinch, where they each grab onto the other at the collar. We see that while they're both martially unschooled they are both ardently determined. It's not hard to see how a show of strength in the form of a pushing contest would ensue, each holding tightly to the other's collar and leaning forward and pushing with all their might. This kind of fight goes on amongst adults as much as it does with teenagers. With tiresome predictability they begin to try to push one another back. This, in the minds of the participants, would determine who is stronger, and to a lesser degree who is heavier (but it could just as easily determine who has better traction under their shoes and more energy to spend).

We've all been audience to or subjected to this wasteful and adolescent programming that tells us that a demonstration of control will put us beyond immediate harm and closer to victory than the person being pushed. Furthermore, the belief is that all this can be accomplished by forcefully walking the other person across an open space and finding a wall to plant them into. This then is the next move: to force the other into an immovable object (like the wall just mentioned) for the sake of hurting them, but also pinning them, again to demonstrate control, and to prevent them from having any space to move away in.

This line of thought, if followed all the way through, ends with the need for the attack to become one of blunt force trauma. The person performing the pin either needs to start throwing punches, or to start slamming the other into the wall repeatedly. It's usually the punch that prevails as a course of action, a thing not hard to accept given the amount of strength and stamina needed to slam a person repeatedly into a stationary object would be heavily taxing: slam them, pull them forward again, re-slam and repeat until they collapse due to being bludgeoned with the wall. In the picture below the photos progress through this process from A to B, C and D. In A tori is grabbed onto by his attacker as is indicated by the arrow showing the direction of uke's force output; in B the dual solid arrows represent the slam into the wall, while the dotted lines in C show uke pulling tori away from the wall to set up the attack again so that the slam can be repeated in D.

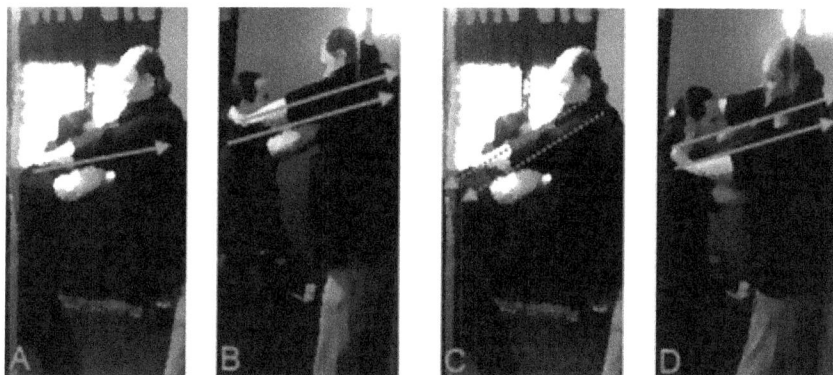

It is true that the person doing the pinning will probably opt to punch before an attempt to win by repeated slamming, but for the sake of this scenario we'll assume the person pinning enjoys enough superiority that they have the necessary strength and stamina to slam the other into surrender. In an everyday brawl the lack of combat education on behalf of both competitors would make punching not quite as recommended by conventional logic as first thought might fancy: unskilled punching probably won't be determinate in the first opening shots, and a decisive outcome will likely require a protracted barrage. To do this the person punching will have to reduce their grip to one hand and give up half their pinning control to the person against the wall who still possesses some ability to move laterally. It takes more energy to punch and miss than punch and hit, and with this said the reader should understand that while punching is the preferred mode of attack by common assailants here, it's by no means energy-conservative or a better gambit for a person who's enjoying a marked strength advantage over the person they've put into that wall. In the absence of that wall, or window or what have you, any object such as parked cars in a lot will serve the attacker in the same capacity.

The combative objective here, like in any scenario, is to win. The pusher here hopes to accomplish this by mounting a repetitive assault in the form of the push-and-slam described above. The question the reader needs to be asking themselves at this juncture concerning this hypothetical engagement is how many push-and-slams, and of what force, are required to create any real victory? The aggressor's desperate, not entirely irrational hope, is that the energy being exerted to put the other person into that wall, over and over, will be enough. How much energy would this require? Not an insignificant amount. How much damage does each slam into the wall yield? That would depend on how much stronger the aggressor was than the person on the receiving end of the attack, but unless there is great disparity in strength the damage won't be catastrophic unless the back of the skull is taking the brunt with each new collision. That means that this tactic of repeated bludgeoning won't mount damage quickly.

So far then the dominant personality has managed to back up his opponent, pin him to the wall, mount an unsophisticated attack (with the benefit of attrition, but at the cost of much energy) and is reaping small returns of gain that are in the process of slowly amounting to damage. Now we have established a common attack with a specific damage as the outcome, as well as having stated the time, energy and conditions needed to make it viable.

Now if the reader will reference the image on next page, we must imagine the Jūjutsu student placed in the same predicament, aiming to achieve the same type of damage but not being restricted by lack of means to accomplish it. Again the collar clinch takes place as before, but now the tactics are different: the Jūjutsu practitioner realizes what is about to happen, that the predictable pushing contest is about to occur. In anticipation of this he begins to push his opponent, but purposefully not enough to dislodge him or push him back. The opponent doesn't know this is calculated, he only believes that the other person isn't as strong and can't push any harder. Now the Jūjutsu student lets himself be pushed backward. First just a step. And then after that a second step. Suddenly he stops pushing altogether and abruptly pulls his opponent forward, into the direction his adversary is pushing: this sets up the hip toss as his opponent is already moving in the right direction and is helpless to stop. The hip toss is totally unexpected and as such has an excellent success rate in this scenario. Uke grabs tori in photo E, and tori replies by returning the clinch in photo F, aggressively pushing uke back for the purpose of baiting the other forward. In photo G uke pushes hard in answer, thrusting forward and taking the bait, not realizing his forward expenditure of energy is a valuable asset to tori's tactics. As uke pushes tori back in photo H, the latter deftly rolls the former over his hip and slams him into the floor.

The wall that uke had relied upon in the common attack to slam tori into is the type of aid that can't be counted upon to be at hand. Without it the one doing the pushing would eventually spend a goodly portion of stamina on a pointless tactic. The Jūjutsu student knows better, however: he isn't looking for a wall to slam his opponent into, he'll use the ground. Under his feet and readily available, the ground (or floor) doesn't have to be looked for or hoped for, just felt underfoot to know it's there. The martial artist knows that far more advantageous than his own strength is proven method, and the method he's chosen to use happens to utilize gravity to affect the slam of the opponent into the ground. These are considerable advantages. The slam into the earth (or worse a concrete floor or asphalt road), is upwards of two to three times harder than a hard push into a wall. If the opponent lands flat on his back (as is expected) he'll be winded and stunned; if he hits his head it may be that he'll require something more than first aid until someone more skilled, like paramedics, arrive.

Whatever is first acquainted with the pavement, his back or his head, either or, there will be a crop of question marks sprouting up in the skull of the person just thrown, the kind of confusion that marks the end of a contest. If it doesn't, the Jūjutsu student now mounts the vulnerable form of his aggressor and begins to enact a second stage plan of attack, a mid-game plan, to facilitate the end of the struggle for good.

In one scenario we see the needless expenditure of energy in the macho tactics that involve pushing the other guy halfway across the parking lot, the preposterous attack using the wall and all the while waiting for it to add up to enough pain and injury to qualify as a win. In the contrasting example the martial artist's energy is spent with an accountant's conscience, and applied with a surgeon's precision. The Jūjutsu student doesn't hope for a nearby wall, but rather uses the ever present ground that doesn't necessitate having to look for it first. He doesn't play the macho-head's push game, but cleverly exploits the other's helplessness to play it. He doesn't waste energy using strength to execute his attack, but uses leverage and lift, and only as much as is needed for gravity to step in and achieve the rest. He doesn't need to pin his opponent to the wall, because the impact of the throw has pinned the other to the floor.

One can see the startling difference between a method that is streamlined and sharp and proven, to something improvised due to panic, pieced together from childhood experiences and that appears almost drunken in action. The empowerment of method will always supersede all other factors, and not simply due to intelligent tactics, but the construction of technique – that merciless and unrelenting order of attack that systematically targets vital points and anatomical weaknesses while jealously protecting its own within layers of reflexive defenses.

D. S. Hopkins

Factor 1: Physiology

Dependent on the type of athletics being discussed, physical advantage can obviously vary in how much effect it'll produce. In certain combat disciplines, such as Sumo wrestling, a heavy mass is required to even effectively use the system of fight being taught. It is designed to purposely utilize weight, which in no way means the heavier sumo wrestlers always win but only that a certain critical minimum is needed to begin. Sumo wrestling has been tested in recent decades against many other modes of fight and has subsequently been forced to acknowledge shortcomings when operating outside of its native tournament environment. Not mass or the ability to use it guarantees superiority in the field - or even in competitions less regulated. Systems of fight such as Kung Fu or Aikido, renowned for speed, are comprised of techniques whose strengths are in their speed of execution; an anatomy that is perhaps thinner and more flexible than most might be able to capitalize on such a combat system faster or a little more effectively – at least at first. The person beside us in the *dojo* who doesn't seem to be as fast or agile because they're not at their ideal weight can lose or gain to change it, yet no amount of manipulation on behalf of our anatomy's characteristics will increase or decrease our combat effectiveness anything like determination and long months of practice will. Boxing and other striking disciplines would be amongst those that benefit from increases in reach and weight, meaning the heavier the striker the heavier the strike, and the longer the reach the farther away it can be used. However, physiology is only as beneficial as the technique able to use it. Some maneuvers will benefit, and some won't. Punches such as the hook and body blow aren't going to experience a betterment from a reach increase like a jab or right cross might for example.

Weight - if not to an obese degree - could be called a natural advantage, and natural advantages are the kind of things that may determine victory in the absence of combat training, the absence of method. As to its advantages, it is not difficult to determine what those might be, but how they can potentially alter the outcome of an engagement when neither combatant has any training to use. We know that larger and heavier people tend to move slower, possessing less dexterity and agility and they may even pay a cardiovascular penalty for their mass, but in disciplines like boxing and kick boxing they can generate more striking power if they're using sound technique. Weight has also the advantage of creating a firmer anchor to the ground, increasing the unlikelihood of being pushed off balance in a tussle. The question is would the increase in power output and the heavier footing make up for the reduction in speed and fluidity of movement? It's difficult to know when considering two persons without combat schooling; and in the event where both people are schooled it becomes a little more important to know what type of martial arts are being represented in the conflict. If, for example, the competitors were both boxers or kick boxers, then one could point out that the authorities that govern such sports definitely believe weight to be a factor because of the weight classification that they've instituted – yet one only needs to look at striking tournaments, MMA or otherwise, where competitors have been matched without weight class restrictions, and then those cases where a lighter combatant proved victorious. If both men were of the same skill with the same excellence of technique, reflexes and conditioning, it would come down to tactics: which techniques were used and how they were used and at what time during the fight, who had the right move at the right time, who miscalculated and used the wrong move at the wrong time and so on. It would ultimately be decided by each fighter's quality of skill and understanding as compared to one another, and then the timing and chosen usage of those techniques in the form of tactics. Weight would certainly contribute to striking power for the persons involved, but not enough to be decisive in of itself.

Both Kung Fu and Aikido are generally remarked to work well with slighter people of middling height, yet people much taller – Steven Seagal is six feet four inches – have risen to the top of globally recognized practitioners. Skeletal structure, height and breadth, are the real constants of a person's anatomical shape and the broad person or the tall person doesn't always find those things an advantage or enhancement. In a particular system of fight or up against a particular system they can work to the disadvantage, but again not decisively.

If anatomy were a definitive factor, it would not be possible to overcome the shortcomings found there. Such physiological considerations, however, factor in less and less as the martial artist becomes progressively more accomplished, until finally skill has made such considerations marginal. It's not uncommon to see two people of the exact same quality and duration of schooling fighting against one another with one considerably larger but still unable to win over the lighter person because of a difference in technique quality, more suitable tactics or intuition. A worthy consideration may not necessarily be to what degree anatomical characteristics will assist the student's practice of certain techniques, but how it could possibly complicate their efforts. Excess weight can make simple cardiovascular exercises much harder than they need to be, an anatomy densely muscled often lacks flexibility and range of motion, and under-muscled people have to rely on an outstanding understanding of technique and the principles it uses to allow momentum and position and leverage do what their musculature can't. Though this last one represents an unimpeachable reliance on sound technique, it may make it much harder to initially learn. All this has only addressed shape and quality of anatomical substance, having left quite aside any consideration that addresses quality of sight or of hearing, balance or of coordination. Luckily, almost everything mentioned here can be overcome, some things with a little effort, others with a lot, but in the end the adeptness of the student using method, technique and tactics will eventually become definitive, eclipsing all else, the positives and negatives, in the pursuit of competence.

It can't be emphasized enough: skill makes winners, and the lack of it makes losers. And all the while each person is directly responsible for how much effort they invest in their own skill sets. You get back what you put in, like everything else.

Any Olympic wrestler, Judo champion or Jūjutsu *Shihan* will tell you that the lower your center of gravity is the easier it is to get it under your opponent and lift him off his feet. People that are shorter would have what could be called a natural physiological advantage in that their centers of gravity are closer to the ground to start with, making it that much easier to get beneath their opponents. But the advantage wouldn't be much unlike a striker's reach, meaning that it would be employable to a degree of benefit in certain techniques and only then if they were sound. The value isn't exactly in the shorter anatomy, but in using it with those maneuvers that will be enhanced by it, and furthermore the usage of those maneuvers in a tactical plan that would make them key to achieving the conditions needed for victory. The shorter person, the lither person, the taller person, and the heavier person must realize that within the study of martial arts these advantages can make certain techniques and tactics easier for them to learn and use, but mustn't be depended upon to be anything other than a minor aid. Small advantages like anatomy may make that decision slightly easier – but only slightly.

With any two athletic endeavors being pursued at the same time there becomes possible a degree of mutual reinforcement, each potentially able to assist the other. This isn't only true between two pursuits such as body building and martial science, but also between martial science and swimming, running or cycling (perhaps more in the latter cases given that endurance is being held in common by both athletic pursuits, and in the martial arts stamina is at least as desirable as strength). There is also a measure of subtraction that becomes possible, a balance that if violated will cause one to undermine the other. Weightlifting will naturally reduce flexibility if one isn't careful and hence range of motion, a condition directly contrary to martial proficiency and a subtraction that would have to be weighed against the benefit of being able to produce higher force output. Equally, if one is weightlifting and practicing Jūjutsu separately there is a real risk that any one joint, muscle, tendon or ligament can be strained, wrenched or sprained (even slightly) due to moving outside the limits of the current range of motion, and that would likely bring the aspirations of someone's body-sculpting to a sudden halt for an interminable period.

There are benefits to cross-training as any martial artist or competitor would tell you, but nothing resembling those popular myths that the laymen and commoners so dearly cherish. The enhancements provided by one discipline or field of athleticism to another, unless an intimate and intrinsic relationship to begin with (perhaps even sharing a common ancestry or parallel one in nature), will be limited at best, and counterproductive at worst. Someone devoted to a bodybuilding regimen may very well take away some valuable flexibility from a practice of Jūjutsu, and a practitioner of Jūjutsu might find the time and energy given to a weightlifting program that's providing a strength increase body-wide well-invested. But sound technique doesn't require strength as much as it might require other things first: things such as balance, coordination, agility, sensitivity, flexibility, accuracy or reflexivity. This would obviously depend on the condition and ability of the person being considered. Some persons will need one or the other more than all the rest, others may not have a serious deficiency in any one regard.

It is my experience that our most precious and irreplaceable resource, the one thing that simply cannot ever be utilized well enough to meet any satisfaction, is not related to physiology but to *time*. It stands apart from every other resource due to the singular characteristic that it's spent at a continuous rate we cannot control, leaving us only with the control of the quality with which it is being spent. That expenditure is life-affecting, not only in direct proportion to the amount of time being spent and what it's being spent on, but also according to what it's *not* being spent on. This is of the greatest import to us as students. To invest ourselves in a track and field regimen, a weight training regimen, calisthenics or swimming laps at the pool is going to require a significant amount of time – and from the perspective of a martial artist, that is time that will need to be taken away from something else. Those places where that needed time will be subtracted from will have to be from the heart of the discipline itself: the philosophy of combat doctrine, from the fundamentals to the complexities of the technical processes; the combat-specific conditioning practices of bone strengthening, limb stretching, reflex building and the cultivation of balance; the anatomical familiarization of joints, tendons, vital points, range limitations and natural weaponry - and then the excruciating commitment to the exhaustive repetition of it all. It is a question truly of the first magnitude that we understand and fully appreciate how much time we have and where it'll be invested. With only so many hours and minutes in a day to use for our ambitions or passions, we must be absolutely sure they are spent serving our best interests at all times.

Most students, athletes, masters or grand masters of martial arts allocate time for the development of physical attributes such as the cardiovascular system or the musculature system, cognizant of the impact of anatomical systems that can perform for a longer period of time and at a higher output than the ordinary; but such things, as beneficial as they are, can by no means be the first concern or the first goals sought by the student of combat. To learn the art itself must be the first priority, and the comprehension of that curriculum must precede all considerations such as becoming stronger, heavier, leaner or faster. These latter attributes, of course, will develop over and in their own time, but supplementing martial practice with an extracurricular commitment is going to require a division of focus and resources, which means we must be very sure before we make such expenditures. It has been a goal of this writer to meet auxiliary objectives like strength or respiratory development by enhancing the martial training regimen itself using ankle or wrist weights, accelerating pace to create conditions to promote cardiovascular goals – all while never allowing focus on the martial training to falter or waver.

The notion that a high proportion of muscle mass will place a massive magnification on combat skill is as reasonable as the notion that the ability to fight will make it far easier to lift weights. A gymnast, a bodybuilder and a marathon runner have about as much chance of beating a martial artist in a fight as the martial artist does of outperforming the gymnast on the pommel horse, the bodybuilder in a dead-lift or the marathon runner in a 42.2 km run. It's the kind of uninformed supposition that ranks with the idea that a marathon runner will make an excellent soccer player because he's good at running. It entirely ignores the necessity of ball control, passing technique and shooting technique all while maintaining the first focus, which is the protection of the ball. The marathon runner's conditioning in itself wouldn't be unhelpful, but it would only be useful if the person had the basic skills of the game in question. Taekwondo requires a great deal of flexibility and balance. Now imagine a male ballerina. They have far more flexibility and far more balance than someone in Taekwondo, but does this mean that a ballerina will win full contact striking tournaments and fend off street attackers? Absurd.

The question as to how much strength is required to begin a study of a combat discipline is not hard to answer, but what is a little more complicated to explain is the effect a physical attribute like strength has on martial practice. To begin a person needs little to nil, and this is because the challenges early on are going to be structured and measured to stay within the ability of the student. To impart the early and essential precepts, the displacements and understanding of bodily limitations, and the introductory techniques, it is most necessary to stay within the student's ability – otherwise the only persons that would possess the ability to perform the maneuvers are those that have extraordinary or freakish natural advantages. While only a very little strength is required to begin, because the opponent's attacks are carefully restrained and controlled, doesn't mean the process of learning is designed to remain that way. Eventually, little by little, the restraints are slowly slackened and this predictably forces the student to work much harder to make the same maneuvers succeed. While strength will be forced to increase as the training unfolds, it will not be the attribute relied upon to perform the maneuvers as it itself will be insufficient to accomplish such a task; the maneuvers will continue to succeed because skill level in the student has been undergoing a steady increase. To accomplish the maneuvers the actual principles of the martial processes must become sharper and faster: a state of being only comprehension and repetition and amelioration can produce. Strength is much like balance, reflex, coordination and stamina: a critical minimum is required, not to learn the art, but to eventually fight with it. These critical minimums could be understood as that smallest amount of reflex, balance, agility, coordination, strength, stamina or flexibility necessary – that *must* be present - for a student to be able to practically execute the maneuver.

If someone begins a practice and is already very flexible, balanced or strong it will be that much easier to learn maneuvers that demand these minimums, but the danger is that such natural ability is seductively easy to become dependent on – a crutch, basically - allowing us to have shoddier technical skill and to make up for it with our innate physiological characteristics. This can be neutralized as a pitfall by forcing the flexible, stronger or faster student into performing the maneuver with greater resistance earlier in the curriculum, and force them away from a potential dependence on bodily advantages. If, on the other hand, someone begins a practice and is uncommonly rigid, unbalanced, or weak it will be more difficult to learn the maneuvers, but the advantage is that the learning will require a heavy emphasis on combat principles and processes, compensating for deficiencies of anatomy with hyper-accurate execution of movements and heightened usage of the art's precepts – assuming the potential capability exists.

The pollution of confusion on the topic gets worse once we're beyond the misguided deliberation of who's stronger, as we now have to consider those who hold the belief that stronger is somehow tied to bigger. Some people nurture the notion that the otiose weight they force their heart and lungs to drag around – regardless of whether it be a minor or major bodily state of excessive mass - will provide them a tactical edge in a violent engagement. This they believe because of an enculturation effect or experiences most of us are exposed to from childhood that lead us to hold lifelong perceptions: bigger things and people are at most times heavier and harder to move, and this can only mean that the larger person experiences the opposite when moving smaller and lighter people. No one is entirely sure how this translates into combat potential, they only feel that it does (or that it should). The most serious flaw in this misperception is that the larger person possesses a strength and energy equal to their size, allowing them not only to move any person of lesser weight, but also ensuring that the slighter person will have an equally difficult time moving them. This ignores the quality of the weight in question. A physique possessing a high quantity of musculature may be capable of an increased force output, yet that doesn't guarantee it'll be able to sustain the effort for any duration or that the effort will have combative viability; anatomies subjected to disproportionate baggage, that taxation that comes with an unhealthy fat-to-muscle ratio, aren't only dispossessed of any higher force output, but in fact may be penalized by a greatly *diminished* strength capability.

The suggestion that the presence of such weight is advantageous betrays a lack of understanding regarding two things: firstly, the nature of hand-to-hand combat, and secondly the nature of slovenly anatomies. The methodologies of most martial arts don't rely on the ability to apply great amounts of direct force against general non-critical targets, meaning that the martial artist isn't going to throw himself into a pushing contest or a tug of war with the heavy guy, the body builder, or even another martial artist. Dependent on the combative methods of his discipline, he will attack using techniques of exactitude and refinement and there will be no wasted force spent anywhere other than the pursuit of the attack or defense. In the type of Jūjutsu that this work is based upon, a set of tactics exists for the advent of someone spending high energy to push the student backward by pushing themselves forward – techniques that not only make direct use of that force being applied, but depend on it. Equally, there are other techniques that depend on the attacker dragging the student forward. It should be noted that the Jūjutsu system used as a reference here is not the only one, and other systems could have answers far more numerous to attacks along the forward-reverse axis. For an opponent to attack using a simplistic expenditure of force pushing forward or hauling back, and having no technical training as to the moves and counter moves that can be initiated from the said position, would be indicative of faulty energy management, essentially trying to carry out the push-and-slam common attack in the photo sets earlier where uke attempted to use the wall.

Even if this type of physical altercation is viewed from a striker's perspective as opposed to a grappler's, the excessive weight carried on the other side of the engagement, be it fat or muscle, would only muck and clutter up one's ability to move fluidly (although this would be great deal more of a hindrance in an overweight person than someone conditioned through bodybuilding) making them more easily targetable. Also the idea of grabbing onto a striker without any combat training, hoping to dismay and neutralize their range will have a better than fair chance of backfiring once the clinch is attempted. Just as grapplers are schooled to close distance, strikers are schooled to keep it open, and that means to get a grip is going to require something more than a desire, but a very real gambit to move into an artillery zone. Many strikers also have close-quarter striking tactics, attacks that subject the opponent to all manner of close range assault, such as elbows and knees and those percussion tactics found in disciplines such as Muay Thai, and unconventional hand strikes.

Grappling onto someone with no clear idea of what the next best move should look like, or what attacks they've inadvertently subjected themselves too, would be from the outset even more perilous. From a grappler's perspective the increase in weight of the obese person would mean that certain lifts and throws would be abandoned for sweeps and balance breakers, chokes and locks. The dense musculature of an anatomically developed person such as a weightlifter will undoubtedly offer a greater resistance capacity to joint locking and manipulation tactics due to the elevated force output, but the protection would only be transient. The reason this would offer only a tenuous insulation against the bone breaks and wrenches of joint are due to the grappler's methodology. The processes don't depend on any direct application of strength to achieve locks and torques on the target joints, but subtleties of process that use division and percussion to weaken targets, and attacks that utilize momentum, leverage, and coordination to secure them. All of these are reliable instruments of submission and breakage, proven in conflict, able to ensnare, lock and destroy limbs many times stronger or thicker than those applying the hold.

The great misapprehension by so many is that the fight between two people will be decided by the winner of the push-pull, tug-of-war...because the tug-of-war, as just about everyone believes, is the fight. And how could anyone win the tug-of-war if they're not the big guy or the fat guy? This represents an outlook that is something of a self-infliction to the faculties of reason. It's not a belief sporadically held, nor is it upheld only by those people whom it flatters, but also by everyone else who not only entertain it and afford it a specific deference, but by doing so deny the actual truth. The presupposition, having been founded on infantile experience and then reinforced throughout adulthood (how many of us ever learn to combat efficiently?), proceeds from those first struggles in the playground, a time and place where the only means was that of natural advantage. Quite simply, no one knew how to struggle effectively against someone else, not by way of wrestling, or punching, or pinning, or locking and all that remained was strength, weight, height and the naturalness of the anatomy's condition. Much the same way a six-year-old will attempt to move a box, by throwing themselves into it and maintaining the push until either it moves or they tire, they also attempt to move other people. This is where it starts: the idea that bigger is better and heavier is better. We end up dragging this misperception through life behind us, like intellectual ballast, ensuring our understanding is never able to rise above those initial elementary experiences, and because most of us never study martial science and never acquire efficiency we rely on the schoolyard lessons as adults: we relive the experiences of youth, and not knowing any better, validate the misperception over and over.

It reveals an inactivity of thought on the matter, one that only education on the topic can rectify, and is surpassed only by the inactivity of physiology that is central to the theme of the criticism.

The lonely advantage that the very heavy opponent clings to – and there is only one – is that mass will convey, as is evident in the case of the Sumo wrestler, a body that is increasingly anchored to the ground as the weight increases. That means that as hard as it'd be for the heavy man (not the Sumo wrestler) to be picked up, thrown or otherwise pushed, it'd be nearly as difficult for him to move his foe as this entails moving himself (an underdeveloped musculature and respiratory pushing his own uncooperative dead weight) in addition to that of his opponent who is actively resisting him. He certainly won't be able to maintain anything even close to an aggressively paced fight due to oxygenation concerns, nor will he have an easy time with such an underdeveloped musculature picking up even a two hundred pound man who is energetically resisting him. Sparring would be particularly difficult as it requires a great amount of stamina. Flexibility would be nigh on nonexistent. Speed, agility and dexterity would be fictional. These are the drawbacks, the actual subtractions to ability that an individual suffering from an overweight status can expect as a trade-off for the 'advantage' of being difficult to move. The notion that they'll be able to move their opponent falls apart when you realize that such a feat will require a protracted necessity for deep and rapid breath.

There is a comedic idea that is sometimes proposed that a body mass index of high fat can't be a disadvantage if Sumo wrestlers exist who are such aggressively active athletes. This fallacy completely ignores everything beyond the obvious, accounting for a surface appraisal and nothing else. When comparing Sumo wrestlers to the typical overweight person, it is important to note firstly the quality of the weight gain itself: these athletes didn't get overweight by accident, but rather it was part of a dietary strategy to calculatedly cover their muscle with the fat. Secondly the type of food ingested is not of the high sugar, high fat, high sodium, low mineral, low nutrient, low carbohydrate, low protein type, but consists of specially formulated recipes to include all nutritional concerns and energy provision for workout sessions. Thirdly, of course, is the workout sessions themselves: a regimen of high energy output to develop techniques that also condition muscle and respiratory systems. Unlike the typical overweight person a *Rikishi* (Sumo wrestler) knows his weight won't win the fight, but that his long training in technique and tactics will – it just happens to be technique that utilizes mass.

Anatomical qualities like mass, strength and size are impressive – but it's an impression made more on the eye and not nearly as much on the body in combat conditions. If size and mass always enjoyed the highest statistical likelihood of winning in no-holds-barred tournaments around the world, then Sumo wrestlers would rule the roost and no one else would have a chance. If a freakish amount of strength could overcome all technique, overcome all tactics and all methodology there would be no martial arts, just an enormous multitude of weight gyms. If endurance alone proved to be the key to victory then all the fighters would spend their days on the track running laps. These things on their own don't win.

The martial arts are an exacting index of methods to attack and defend, and no amount of gymnastic flexibility, strength training, cardiovascular conditioning, or ballerina balance is going to make someone immune to the human body's vulnerabilities or be able to weaponize the body, to use it to attack and defend with any efficiency or authority in the absence of schooling. There is a sense-driven and verifiable rationale as to why martial artists, in the *dojo* and those in the professional combat sports, invest their time in a meticulous training regimen that favors firstly combat techniques and tactics, and then a highly specific allotment of time into the various conditioning programs thereafter. In such a precisely crafted training regimen the conditioning being gained is being carefully cultivated to support certain skill sets. Conversely, method without mass, strength, speed, respiratory development, balance, coordination, agility, reflex, or judgment is only knowledge without bodily support or expression. All these things (and more) are needed to begin to use a method of attack and defense like that taught within the realm of the martial sciences, but without the method itself, without the science of application and process, all these attributes are for nothing – it is the art itself that teaches us how to use them. It all comes down to 'how'.

In the martial sciences, as in athletics in general, methodology will always overcome physiology, and this is probably one of the greatest truths connected to the study of martial arts. With methodology being the determining factor in any engagement, technique and tactics, we have identified and weighed the first contributing factor: physiology. And it represents only one contributory factor of those that exist, but there are others that will play in against the scales to attempt to affect the outcome, most a little less, some a little more.

Factor 2: Armament And Armor

The effect of armament and armor can't be dismissed as game-changing factors. In very particular cases it wouldn't be untrue to attribute the word decisive to the influence of arms and body-protective agents. Decisive is a word that demands the most careful usage, and is here used with such care as it could alter the outcome of a violent altercation under special conditions. A firearm for instance could create one such condition. It would be a harder condition for a knife to create as the weapon is limited to the speed of the attacker, as well as his reflexivity and force output. Many martial art *dojos* teach counter knife maneuvers. That's not to say a knife can't be decisive, only that it isn't nearly as likely as a firearm. The list of weaponry here could unfold on and on, from hatchets and axes to sling shots and chains. This would prove a long and cumbersome affair, to speculate on each various weapon and the proposed tactics to counter it, made longer by the fact that some would be unconventional and being so stray outside the bounds of what is typically available or expected. This would mean they'd have to be treated as though they were the next closest thing, familiar weapons or objects similar in shape, size and weight.

Some of the more creative enhancements in the way of arms are in relation to brass knuckles, heavy rings that emulate them, a roll of coins in the fist or a combination lock with its white metal hoop covering the third finger. This introduces an aspect of stealth to the armament dilemma, making it possible to be ambushed – a danger every bit as dire as being clubbed while turning a corner. Though these weapons present themselves as adolescent in sophistication they compensate for their lack of power with a state of near-invisibility while wrapped within the fist. It's not easy to speculate on such tactics and how they'd factor in to the outcome of a fight, considering that if the weaponized enhancement is detected it loses the element of surprise and the greater part of its likelihood to do injury. Trying to compute the odds of a martial artist detecting it seem pointless given the focus of a person could be affected by almost anything and depends on how well the weapon was concealed. Disciplines more orientated to countering and using weaponry would certainly pick it right out.

The real danger when talking about concealable weapons (outside of a small handgun) is indisputably a short knife, which would indeed be a grave threat. By combining stealth with the destructive power of sharpened steel we arrive at the creation of a threat that cannot be taken lightly regardless of our training. The brighter side of this story is that most weapons are not concealable, and outside of short knives and fist enhancements all others are going to be most likely detected – and that means that a great part of their effectiveness is lost in detection. A necessary observation to point out here is that the attacker wielding an unseen weapon would most likely only get the one surprise attack before the advantage was detected and lost – the question is whether or not his opening attack would succeed, and if it did, the next question would have to be whether or not it was critical. It could be argued that once the weapon is identified and the martial artist prepares for it the advantage is once again his, but while it's invisible to him there may almost be something like an equal degree of danger to each: the unschooled attacker, armed and undetected against the schooled combatant who is unarmed and unaware.

As for the firearm threat, it's complicated, and as expected the worst of the lot. This topic of discussion was already broached in *Chapter 7: Threat Assessment: Classification of Tactics, Weaponized Attacks*, and so there is very little to add here. The advantages conferred by a firearm to a hostile personality are immense. A schooled combatant, even one trained in methods of disarm, would need optimum conditions for any kind of attempted disarmament. Before that scenario is delineated here though, what would be of crucial importance is the ability of the gunman. There is as much difference between a first degree black belt in Jūjutsu and an unschooled thug on the street as there is between that same thug armed with a gun and a serving police officer. If the gunman in our scenario isn't a police officer or ex-military, he may have no previous marksmanship training and only a desire to inflict bodily harm and his aim might be worthless outside of ten feet. If he's an inexperienced hoodlum then it's also possible he could be anything from a crack head to a jacked up and jumpy meth-head, or he could be searching for his next fix shaky and unsure – this quality of shooter may even leave the safety engaged, or the weapon unloaded. Quite irrespective of the shooter's apparent state of mind and body, the firearm demands we take the threat seriously and at full face value. In our scenario landscape plays a not insignificant role. Is there cover to take if he starts squeezing off rounds? This will alter the dynamic. How close is he when he pulls the weapon? Close enough to reach? For a disarm technique to function it requires proximity, positioning and mastery – with all lesser factors preferably optimum and in our favor. It's a lot to ask, and every bit is needed. If these conditions are met however, then the odds of prevailing might be fair. Someone with trigger experience will commit no such errors or lapses in judgment. A trained marksman, much like a martial artist, will be attempting to provide himself the most favorable conditions to achieve victory – or at the very least to achieve superiority.

Armor may seem absurd, but only at the very first. We actually wear armor every day, the difference being that clothing is protecting us from the elements more than anything else. The only real defensive value clothing has in a physical engagement, even the heaviest and most durable fabrics, would be to absorb the cutting edge of a knife. Any knife worth its weight will cut through cotton and polyester and skin and tissue without the attacker even detecting a transition from one to the other. Denim or leather may prove more of a chore for the blade, and though the knife will cut through it the slash may not be quite as deep in the skin beneath as it would most certainly be with lighter fabrics. It wouldn't be worth attacking someone wearing a denim shirt under a heavy leather or winter coat where those garments provide coverage. It's not hard to see how fast the best targets would become head and neck for cutting attacks. This doesn't neutralize thrusts, or impaling attacks, the same way but it does reduce an attacker's options. In this particular example the defender is the one who is benefiting from the synthetic enhancement, whereas in every other instance the enhancement was deliberately given to the attacker so that we could gain a small idea of how it would alter his chances against the martial artist. The reason the scenario here is reversed and the martial artist is assumed to be using the armor is because the heaviest and most durable fabrics are substandard shock absorbers – useless against a martial artist's attacks, and only have any real tactical value as a small impediment to the knife's cutting edge. Multiple layers of heavy clothing such as leather may cause a fractional reduction in cutting power. To proceed as in the prior examples and give the attacker in this scenario the benefit of the armor and make the martial artist the one attacking with a knife edge creates an entirely foregone conclusion: we'd have to assume the martial artist will ignore the covered parts of the body and start systematically attacking every exposed vein and artery. The fight would be over before it started.

There is such a thing as real armor for the type of combat we're talking about, and it's routinely employed by SWAT (Police: Special Weapons And Tactics) as well as other security trades and no doubt by any modern military, whether they be infantry or of other specializations. An excellent example of such armor is products that employ nomex or kevlar, with fire or cut resistant properties. These types of products are widely available, but like the armorial protection of civilian clothing will not absorb the kind of shock that a expert in hand-to-hand could level at it (unless, of course, it be a vest designed for anti-firearm use). Even if the protection were highly shock absorbent it would still provide little or no protection against the types of torque, torsion and extenstion techniques a Jūjutsu student will use.

Factor 3: Environment

Environmental conditions are almost always overlooked as variables that could complicate the outcome of a fight: whether it's about to happen on the sidewalk in front of the bar at three in the morning; in the trail that shortcuts across the field to the convenience store on a rainy night; in the parking lot at the mall on Christmas Eve; on the job site on a July afternoon, it could make something nasty to begin with even worse. No one considers the impact the weather, the time of day or night, month of year or geographical location will have on the violent physical contest about to happen. If two people are about to find themselves at odds in the late hours of the night, like outside the local bar at three a.m. as mentioned above, the specific traits of the area will suddenly go from uninteresting to most important. A small club or bar on a slow day of the week will mean that the two about to engage one another may be without spectators of any kind - now if things get out of hand no one is there to intervene for good or for ill. Bad or non-existent street light on top of sub-standard eyesight may very well mean that those eyes don't see the short knife that's in the opponent's hand.

Not to be overlooked is weather. If there's heavy rainfall in the trail that cuts across the field as you're walking it, and this happens to be where Ole Triple J decides to surprise tackle you for what you said regarding the flags he uses as curtains, and the fight becomes a grasp and clinch tussle, you might want to be cognizant of the fact that water can be slippery, and more so when it's combined with sweat. What's worse is that clothes tend to severely restrict movement the wetter and clingier they get. On the one hand there's a reduction in gripping quality and potential, on the other there's a hindrance to range of motion, and rain also affects not only long range visibility, but also short range if the precipitation is heavy enough for it to splash into the face and eyes. But now you're finding out - never needing to have considered it before - that the worst part of this trail is its slipperiness, the mud is so greasy that you can't get any sure footing. Granted, these factors are hardly enough to really alter the outcome of anything, except in extraordinary circumstances; yet, they're worth noting if for no other reason than to be reminded that they exist.

As some hoodlum attempts to mug you for your wallet in the mall parking lot on Christmas Eve, the fat heavy snow fall isn't soaking into the ground like the rain in the field had, nor is it causing the kind of slippery skin that complicates gripping (it would be unusual for combatants to be bare skinned in a snowfall anyway), but what it does allude to is the temperature: if it's cold enough to snow it's cold enough for water to freeze. You notice the frozen puddle from a tiny sheen of light reflecting off it, the mugger doesn't. The puddle is even a little camouflaged by that fresh powder that's on it. A side kick is powerful and effective on dry ground, it may be far greater if the person who received it was without any traction at all – it would take them clear off their feet.

If you were standing on a job site in late July when the other contractor begins to mouth off at you for no other reason than adolescent machoism or a latent insecurity, and now perceives a chance to be center-stage on the adult playground, then already the environment demands certain considerations. Imagine also that you don't want to hurt him, only deflate him a little. A push ensues, then a tussle. You drop on purpose, wrap his one leg with both of yours and begin a *heel hook* to torque his ankle. You decide to crank the ankle just enough to make him screech. You twist the ankle over, begin to torque, but it's only half-effective. The steel toed boots he is wearing are high cut – too high - they're covering the ankle and reducing the poignancy of the lock. Sure you could move on to a different maneuver, but how supremely frustrating would that be? We must take note of our environment, how it affects us and how it effects the other guy.

The prevailing environmental conditions, from time of year to time of day, can be all important to technique. Most maneuvers, though implementable at any time, might be all the more effective if certain characteristics are present: such as long sleeve shirts. If a grappling technique functions best when controlling a clinch at the opponent's wrist, then a long-sleeve shirt would be a desirable garment for the grappler to work with. And the stronger the fabric the better the clinch: winter would all but guarantee such a clinch point, while spring might only see the other with a wind-breaker that will tear under stress. While it's relatively safe to assume some sort of clothing will be present, and this makes training with a *gi* (or uniform) a prudent policy, it should be noted that there may be no opportunity for clinch points on fabric-based materials if the person is shirtless. Summer would reduce the maneuver to attempting to control the person at the sweaty, slippery wrist. It's a strange truth that our environment could cause certain maneuvers to end up under headings that could very well be seasonal - *winter* and *summer* for example - given that one technique might require the foe to have heavy clothing on that we can grab onto to perform a throw, while another maneuver requires the ankle to be unprotected by anything like a high-cut heavy winter boot that would have covered the joint, and so the sandals and sneakers of the summer season make the technique more viable and easier to use. Even ambiance would alter which maneuvers might work better or worse in certain sightless conditions: grappling techniques just might prove better suited to fight without sight using touch alone for guidance once the clinch is established. Spatial limitations, like a tight alley, with little room to move that sees four people converging on us from different directions would constitute a mass attack scenario where the speed of striking techniques might prove trustier than anything else.

Ultimately, regardless of misfortune, the maneuvers need to be able to function under difficult conditions that offer little to no support, even in a climate that is convoluted with a wealth of complications. Everything concerning environment, though expounded on, long and true, regarding terrain or visibility or traction should be accounted for. The acquisition of expertise in anything means a study of details, because if we're aware of the smallest factors, chances are we've taken account of the larger ones. Expertise is in no small way determined by thoroughness.

Factor 4: Mindset

With these minor factors having been weighed, there remains but one last to consider. It is this last factor of mindset that influences the outcome for better or worse, that is the greatest threat and greatest ally, best modification to methodology, and the worst sabotage. Mindset can make a person fearless, can make them cower, make them pause or make them rush; it can inflict defeat or bestow victory, the posture of thought alone.

Mindset and its intimate relationship to morale have been a subject of obsession of militaries since time immemorial. The reason is obvious enough: troop combat initiative is all but decided by attitude. If a solider, or worse yet an army of them, doesn't believe they can win a battle and hence don't even try when they're signaled to charge but instead break and run in the other direction, the best methodology in the world can't help them if they're not willing to use it. It represents the most perilous kind of influence on the outcome of a combative engagement, not only because it's responsible for how the soldier will fight, but also responsible for whether he will or not. Mindset is unique because of this. Complicating the effect of mindset is that it is most inconstant, ever in a state of susceptibility to flux. This means any other stimuli or event can alter it at any other time. Stated like this it's not hard to see why military establishments become fixated with morale and the mindset that maintains it; this formula of preparing a combat force for what it's likely to encounter deeply affects the performance of that force.

The difference between being surprised and being prepared is often decisive, not only between singular combatants, but also between entire formations of combatants. One can't help but wonder about the collective mentality of the Samurai at Hakata Bay in 1274 when the Mongols landed: here is an otherwise prepared Japanese military encountering tactics just unexpected enough to create shock amongst their troops, and with it surely that onset of doubt that necessarily follows. Historically, the Samurai were expert archers in their own right, but for the short days that followed the Mongol beach landing in 1274 they were relentlessly targeted by indiscriminate veils of arrow-fire, shot en masse, as the mainland invaders drove them back. Driven and harried inland, looking back on it from the present, it's difficult to believe that the Samurai morale hadn't been damaged. It must've certainly been shaken: homes and structures set ablaze by a pursuing enemy.

The Mongol invader, we've been told, returned to their ships as night fell and were subjected to a weather system, a gale force wind, that sank or destroyed a great part of the Mongol fleet. With that invasion thwarted by stormy sea and sky, the Samurai set about fortifying Hakata Bay against any future incursions. Imagine the mindset (and subsequently the morale) of the Samurai that found themselves back on that beach again seven years later in 1281 when the same invader returned: only now the bay was not without fortifications and uninformed defenders – now it was as ardently protected by preparedness as the minds of its defenders were by their past experience. They knew precisely what they were up against the second time. Though the challenge from their Mongol invaders was far stiffer in character the second time, one has to believe that the readiness of the Japanese mindset had been hardened and their morale buttressed as a result.

History is replete with records of battles won and lost, some of which determined the development of civilization, because one side had a morale advantage, a desire and belief that was stronger and allowed for a greater endurance and exertion. Whenever this happens it most often allows the side with the superior mindset to perform remarkably better than what could have been typically expected. The proverbial 'battle of wills' is descended from such preoccupations of tactics and the understanding of how *will* affects the fight or flight response. It's contribution to a person's capacity for continuance can't be overstated and defies all attempts to be quantified in observable effect.

Much needs be said on behalf of focus, not only our ability to fix our attention on a single, undeviating goal, but one that builds confidence and positivity of outlook instead of one that by its very nature reinforces an attitude of inadequacy, especially when such self-doubt is unfounded. Focus must be used to coordinate the effort of mind and body to work at the most optimum levels and so provide the best performance we're capable of. Such successful action needs to be protected from any undue sense of self-inadequacy or lack of confidence in our abilities. This danger represents that most insidious of enemies – doubt. This is perhaps the worst kind of all as it enters our psyche and sabotages us from within. Doubt doesn't only translate into a loss of momentum, mental or otherwise, but more importantly could be brought about by such a loss of drive. Once the combatant has allowed his mind to become bogged down and even stagnated in unwholesome thought processes, the immediate risk is that the shapeless and melancholy brooding which is born from a preoccupation with stresses and fears begins to subtly grind away at our confidence. Morale is closely related to confidence, and the degeneration of the latter means the same outcome for the former.

Mindset's greatest influence isn't really on methodology itself, but on the person using the methodology. The threat isn't so much that their technique or tactics will suffer, but their will to fight will be destroyed, without which even the mightiest of techniques and tactics is useless. If a person enters into a fight and is unsteady, afraid, or harboring self-doubt this will most certainly affect their execution of technique and implementation of tactics, but the effect would be small by comparison to the danger of losing the will to fight altogether. Yet it happens all the time, that one side, one fighter begins to self-doubt and then before long they're questioning their own techniques, tactics and strategy, convincing themselves as they go along that none of them is good enough, they themselves aren't good enough and that the odds are against their success. Then they fail. With so much of their attention redirected from the critical task at hand to the unproductive pursuit of pondering doubt and inadequacy, the entire combat focus becomes a discontinuous mess of divergent cares and woes. A sabotaged self-esteem then becomes self-validating, ending with thoughts and words like, "I was right to doubt myself, and to prove it I lost." Watching someone inflict this on themselves afterward is hard to bear as they never really face the hard truth that their attitude itself contributed so generously to their defeat, and then they use that defeat to justify the self-doubt that created it. What makes this especially ugly and unbearable is when the defeat was minor and the result of a very close contest, where a hair's breadth of energy applied in the other direction could have tipped the scales back into their favor.

As to the question of effect that this has on martial art methodology, it shouldn't be allowed to affect it with undue undermining, meaning that there will always be some need to prove the skill of the students to themselves. This is typical, even expected, but the average combat discipline should have gone far out of its way to minimize this lack of confidence as much as possible by introducing within the training program an exercise to constantly buttress the confidence of those practicing the discipline (sparring would work well). This preparation would be ideally formulated to use not only sparring, but also scenario-based training in conjunction with improvisation practice, to construct the widest arrays of possibility for each scenario and thus begin a repository of experience in a controlled environment. The reason the above practices are recommended to combat low self-esteem and self-doubt on behalf of the student is because the shape their fear and self-perceived inadequacy will take on will be of personal inability. An inability to carry out successful attack and defense. Any instructor cognizant of these realities, of the kind of stiff and inflexible challenges likely to be encountered, and of the dangerously fragile self-confidence that most students arrive at the *dojo* with, should institute policies to address these inadequacies and anticipated engagements. Scenario based training is a reliable schooling instrument to answer both these needs, and sparring or free practice as well. This beautifully minimizes surprises in the field and provides the student a multitude of answers, which alone provides confidence. Preparation is one of the very best methods to counter demoralization or the undermining caused by self-doubt.

Even without the benefit of scenario based training that seeks to familiarize the student with the grimmer possibilities and so prepare them, the student's mindset is still buttressed by the confidence of a vast combat education, and specifically by the improvisational aspects of that training. The instructor's preparation (or lack thereof), even without the scenario based experience, is clearly crucial: those personalities that had a particularly weak self-esteem, or in some cases completely non-existent, would be the ones most at risk from a disruption of mindset, and an assailing of self-doubt. Those personalities have to be identified early so their inadequacies can be addressed and corrected. If not, their implosion under duress would be predictably higher than their classmates. The beginning of the best defense concerning such mental and emotional frailties is firstly awareness, and secondly the action taken based on that awareness to edify the martial artist and prepare them for the worst.

With that firmly said, we can now turn our attention to that which occurs when all the preparations have been made and the unthinkable still manages to happen nonetheless: we're confronted with a threat that we have no basis in experience for. What if the martial art methodology you've studied and practiced and trusted your life in is challenged by a person in a mindset that can't be reasoned with, intimidated or quelled by pain? Someone hissing and clawing at you in a rage is one thing, but someone actively trying to kill you in an energized frenzy is quite something else. When people are afraid or angry, as such happens when cornered, they are most unpredictable, most violently inclined, and most desperate. Pain compliance is used throughout law enforcement and the security profession and armed forces in the hand-to-hand schooling to achieve submission, but here we're going to introduce an element that removes the possibility of using pain as a motivator to force the other side into surrender. Under adrenaline many people will not submit to what a classmate might have in the *dojo*, won't give up the way we ourselves might have in training, and that means that desperation can directly affect how much resistance you're likely to encounter, and the quality of that resistance and how ferocious it might be.

What if the mindset in question was under the influence of even something more than adrenaline? What if the mindset in question was under the influence of something far more mind-altering? Like the kind of modification that is made by cocaine or worse. Imagine a drug-modified mindset under the influence of adrenaline, brought on by anger and desperation. Imagine pain compliance no longer elicits behavioral value because the subject is either not registering pain, physical damage or psychological shock such as fear, or is only registering it on a diminished level.

Now imagine the following scenario: It's night and winter in an isolated place where the terrain is unknown. No assistance is forthcoming. No one knows where you are. The attacker is making a sincere attempt to kill you. To lose now is to die.

A massive arsenal of techniques can turn the human body into a weapon, but seven tenths of it are useless in this scenario because of the heavy reliance on pain compliance or the presupposition that fear can be induced. The only form of metric in this ugliest of scenarios is actual measurable physiological damage.

Consider that.

That means that breaking the attacker's leg with a power roundhouse kick, the kind used in Muay Thai and *Kyokushin* Karate may stop him, but then it also may not; if it does it won't be due to pain or discomfort. This raises the question of how much structural damage a leg could absorb before failing to support the anatomy it's connected to - because that's what will need to happen. The amount of damage to completely destroy a limb is going to far outweigh the damage needed to hurt most people enough to stop or subdue them. In fact, it may require an amount of energy that simply isn't economical to spend. It may require up to forty or fifty power roundhouses to destroy the bone structure sufficiently to stop the chemically-enhanced attacker. It's no longer merely an energy concern, but there exists a real threat that he'll find an advantage long before you can destroy his ability to advance. This may now demand that the limited energy reserves be utilized against a critical target, like the head. This of course entails a risk of killing the attacker when only immobilization was sought. The first moral obstacle is before us. In the interest of technicality he'd be just as dead if the leg were destroyed in the middle of a winter wasteland – he'd freeze. But it does make clear the dilemma that an environment like winter creates. There are readers who'll insist that the expiry of the freakish attacker is infinitely preferable to the expiry of us ourselves. That is so, and only too true. But it's much easier said than done. And in this particular scenario no easy answer of a combative nature exists: for safety sake we must assume that most martial arts and their respective arsenals of maneuvers will have but a select set of techniques and tactics that will be sufficiently suited for the task at hand. Nor is it discounted that we ourselves could be grabbed or otherwise clinched during a technique and be bit or have our eyes gouged out.

It is the one hypothetical situation where the greater part of the martial artist's maneuvers are either removed from contention or so diminished in combative efficacy that they might as well be removed. If no amount of bone, muscle, ligament or even organ damage is sufficient, what tactics are left to us to combat the threat with? Those techniques will need to be of the variety that does not depend on pain compliance to alter the target's behavior, and that immediately leaves us with maneuvers that cause highly specific outcomes. Throws or balance breakers can allow us to forcibly move the attacker without the need for pain compliance, even if it means accepting the likelihood that we will become locked in a clinch with them (which is not a position we want to enter into without forethought); striking techniques that produce the kind of catastrophic damage to induce a knockout, compromise equilibrium or leave the target sightless by attacking the ocular organs would be valuable as they can potentially achieve these things while keeping distance open; choke holds and strangles that cut off blood or oxygen are surefire maneuvers to disable or destroy an assailant utterly. All these types of maneuvers represent the use of tactics that avoid pain compliance in favor of inflicting an injury or unconsciousness that induces system-wide inoperability, or at the very least a decreased ability of the enemy to function combatively, reducing the threat to a negligible status.

While the particular mode of Jūjutsu from which experience is being drawn on here is stocked with striking maneuvers capable of carrying out the blunt force attack to the jaw or temple to induce the knockout, it really is far better equipped to deal a choke hold, any number of which – guillotine, reverse guillotine, scissor chokes or blood chokes - could attain the required result. The tactics supporting the application of the choke, to achieve the positioning and then actuate the hold would be the hardest to employ, as all pain inducing modes of attack are rendered ineffective, forcing the martial artist to rely on subtlety more than injury and fear.

What the Japanese martial arts refer to as 'no mind,' or *mushin*, is the ability to act or react with unconscious speed to a combat situation, a speed that doesn't require deliberation of what the next move should be. This is a sought after mindset concerning the creation of reflex reactions. Due to the nature of the hypothetical threat constructed above, however, the need for highly specific tactics negates this mental posture of 'no mind' and forces the martial artist to calculate his improvisations on the spot.

A successful defense could undoubtedly be carried out despite this need to use limited maneuver types, and I believe even without loss of life, which is an amazing statement when considering the extremely difficult conditions the martial artist would be set in conflict with. The one chief advantage outside of methodology that the martial artist enjoys in this scenario is the ability to think clearly and strategize, which is a posture of thought the attacker is in all likelihood without, cognition reduced, perhaps even to something like instinct alone. This belief that it could be not only won but done so with a favorable resolution isn't held without the assumption that certain necessary conditions are present: the correct techniques would need to be utilized, such as right crosses, elbow strikes and power roundhouses for striking assets, and all manner of choke holds for grappling assets and particularly escape maneuvers that are responsible for breaking any attempted clinch our opponent may try to make. It would also be necessary that the student have been educated as to how to make the determination that the attacker was temporarily immune to pain and fear inducements, how to qualify his ability to maim or kill us, and then proceed with the prescribed counter tactics – which is the goal of inflicting unconsciousness or a general condition of inoperability.

The chemically altered mindset represents one of the most unique challenges and one of the most isolated in likelihood; the firearm represents the most dangerous of challenges; and the emotionally turbulent person, behaviorally altered with alcohol is one of the most likely instigators of violence. Yet due to the handicap inflicted on the alcohol-intoxicated attacker, his heightened aggressiveness is a self-defeating thing, not explored here as any real threat to the martial artist's methodology. Anger and fear and desperation are probably the most common mindsets that will have to be contended with, and while the chemically-altered pain immunity is not present, adrenaline and reflex and calculatory thought process *is* present, which is a threat and danger all its very own.

Chapter 9

Techniques

The three techniques included here in this last chapter are from the system of Jūjutsu this book uses as its chief point of reference and experience. These three were carefully chosen to allow the reader to appreciate the degree of difference between the maneuvers themselves, as well as to make apparent the degree of difference within each of three major Jūjutsu systems now practiced globally: Jūjutsu, Aiki-Jūjutsu and Brazilian Jiu Jitsu. None of the three are short enough to fall into the prior minimal categorization, nor are they long enough to fall into the chain profile, nor is variability demonstrated in any of them. All three are standardized length and are highly practical, but perhaps most importantly is that you could probably find all three of these maneuvers in any Jūjutsu, Aiki-Jūjutsu or Brazilian Jiu Jitsu system – this is a statement of paramount importance. It underlines the strength of relationship, but far more the strength of origins, between all three. Each of these is unarmed and as so not in the weaponized category, and given that they are a part of a martial system they're innately specialized and never common.

This style of Jūjutsu, which is to say one in a Japanese mode that has been heavily influenced by current period needs, yet retains elements of the classic architecture, places emphasis on taking vertical control (or control from an upright posture on the feet) of the engagement with joint manipulation tactics and focuses on maintaining that control. In this way it bears a strong resemblance to the more modern modes of traditional Japanese Jūjutsu and Aiki-Jūjutsu, but still has access to those more intrinsic ground mechanics that have come to be recognized as a core element of Jūjutsu, firstly by Judo and secondly by that which was developed by Brazilian thought and innovation in their own form of Jiu Jitsu. It needn't be said that a clear impression of a style of fight can't be made with a handful of techniques on a few dozen pages, but perhaps a small glimpse of the system's character can be communicated this way.

The first technique displayed is one commonly seen in Jūjutsu schools and uses cervical torquing, or neck control. This maneuver is popularized in all manner of dramatic visual entertainment, television and film, as that ever-recognizable characteristic neck-snap that is used to quickly dispatch the person whom it is being used on. While this is possible, and very dangerous, the technique of cervical control appears exactly the same, only done much slower. It's a useful and powerful maneuver if taught carefully and practiced that way. It is done with very little force and is delineated in the following image set.

Fig 13.0 Uke grabs tori in the common two-handed collar clinch.

Fig 13.0

Fig 13.1 Tori reaches toward uke and prepares to counter-clinch him: he will create his own clinch at the head exclusively, particularly at the back of the head and the chin. In the dotted line we can see the travel path of tori's far-side hand as it aims for the chin of uke.

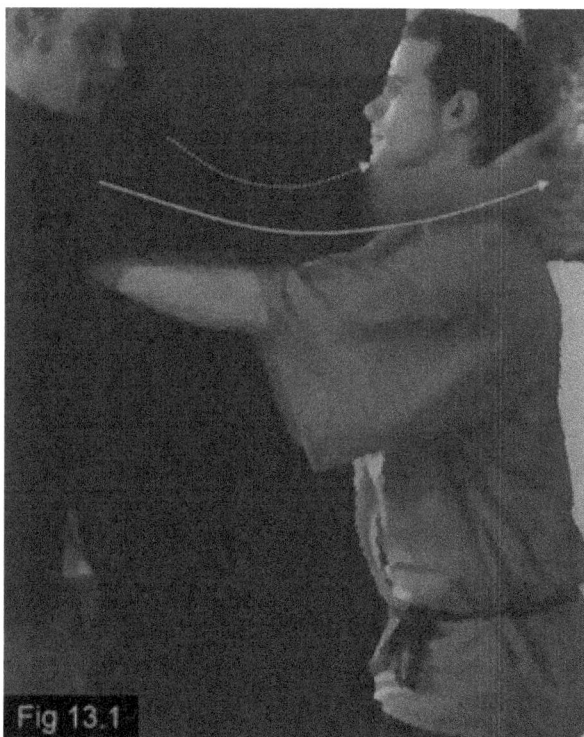

Fig 13.1

Fig 13.2 In this image tori twists the neck of uke clockwise (it works precisely the same going counter clockwise), and then simply turns into the direction which the head is being spun. The two flow arrows are used to demonstrate the torquing force here.

Fig 13.2

Fig 13.3 In this figure tori can be seen now in line with uke, still spinning in the same direction that the head of uke is being torqued. At this stage uke's balance is all but broken, his legs unable to get beneath his center of gravity because of the nature of the twisting force: as it pulls his center out of alignment it subsequently keeps it out of alignment as long as that force is maintained. Uke is trying to stumble backwards, his legs unable to catch up to the rest of his body.

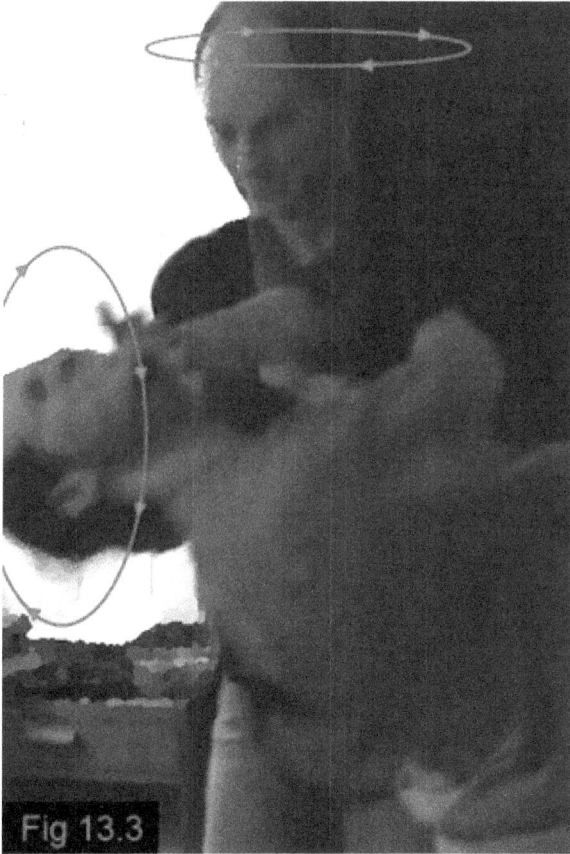

Fig 13.3

Fig 13.4 Uke's balance, now completely negated, sees the maneuver
approaching its end with tori in easy control of the outcome. This represents
a mode of counter-attack often seen in traditional and more contemporary
Jūjutsu styles: moves and counter-moves made from the vertical posture that
controls the engagement from the outset through a rapid reaction mentality
and method. Once uke has fallen another joint lock or critical strike can be
used to reach a definite finality.

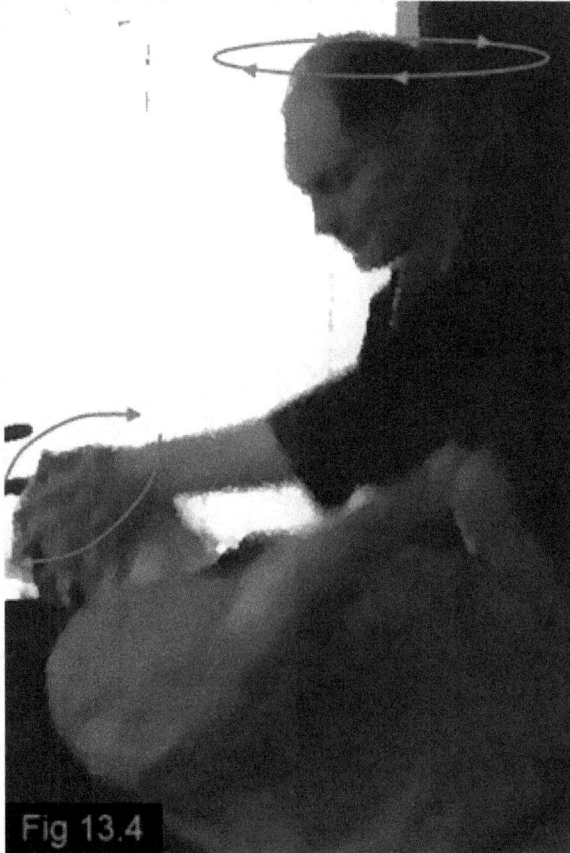

Fig 13.4

Fig 14.0 The second example is probably more indicative of Aiki-Jūjutsu's preference for vertical orientation and the use of interception and redirection, usually through locking and torquing the joints within the arms. Uke attacks with a punch (a reach or thrust functions the same, as do almost any linear move of the arm by uke, such as a finger poke or shove), tori deflects it with his right hand and clasps onto the wrist.

Fig 14.0

Fig 14.1 Tori prepares to begin the entwine which will necessitate his arm crossing over uke's and then dropping down over it.

Fig 14.1

Fig 14.2 Tori begins the first part of a locking maneuver that sees the ensnarement of uke's offending arm by firstly dropping his own armpit over it while pulling it close to the body so it can't withdraw to safety. The arrow indicates the path tori's hand will need to follow to create the reinforced clasp.

Fig 14.2

Fig 14.3 Tori very nearly has completed the threading here: his hand will soon clinch his own opposite wrist, thus completing the clasp.

Fig 14.3

Fig 14.4 Tori's traveling hand has clasped about his right hand's wrist, which will signal the beginning of the next move to actuate a lock, and then from there use that lock to create a throw.

Fig 14.4

Fig 14.5 In this image tori has completed the reinforced clasp and we can take a moment to identify the subtleties of the hold. Letters have been used to identify each of this hold's salient features: at letter A we see tori's left hand, that which has performed the ensnarement and the threading to make the clasp; letter B points to tori's right hand, that which has clinched uke's wrist at the very beginning of uke's attack, and now has bent uke's hand at the wrist and caused his fingers to splay open and his palm to bend at a ninety degree relation to his forearm, pushed back towards the soft underside of his wrist; and letter C points to uke's open fingers, showing the position of the fist that is now an open hand and securely trapped.

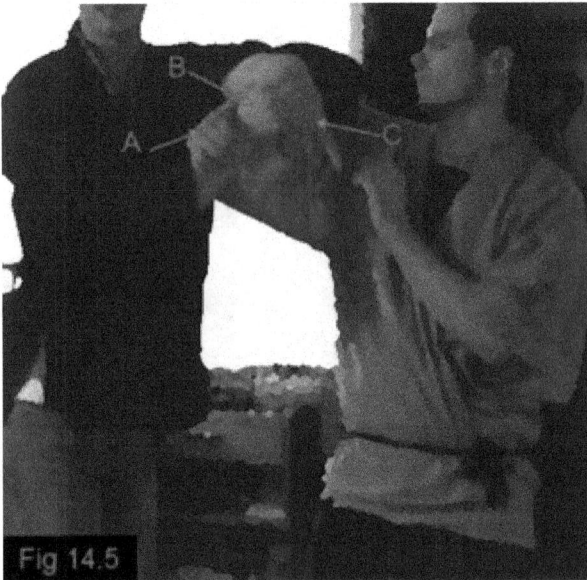

Fig 14.5

Fig 14.6 Here tori has turned into uke, facing him square on and brought the lock to stand upright between them. Much clearer is the sight of uke's open hand, the fist having been forced open by tori's clasp, applying heavy folding force. The circle of arrows indicates the direction tori has moved from and where he wants to continue to go, which will be to the outside of the locked arm, in this case to his own left (or uke's right) and turn counter clockwise to the floor.

Fig 14.6

Fig 14.7 Tori begins the fast counter clockwise rotation, the folding forces against uke's wrist now forgotten in the face of new torquing forces at the shoulder that are pulling him in a tight circle in the direction the arrows are moving.

Fig 14.7

Fig 14.8 Following the circle eventually breaks uke's balance, not much unlike the neck twist in the first technique of this chapter, only that here it's the shoulder's ball and socket joint which is the main motivator. Uke falls straight back and can in no way prevent the fall, following the arrow to the floor.

Fig 14.8

Fig 14.9 Uke is down. The lock is still held by tori and the clasp is as tight as it was a second before. The shoulder is still susceptible to moderate torquing forces from here, but the carpals of the wrist are particularly vulnerable to the previously mentioned folding forces. "A" points to the clasping hand of tori, while "B" is the actual clinching hand.

Fig 14.9

The last technique that will be depicted is a hip toss and arm lock (or *O Gushi* and Kansetsu Waza), and represent that inclination and adeptness at controlling the engagement by moving it downward to the horizontal position and there concluding it. This maneuver is much more aligned to the expertise of the Brazilian schools of thought on Jiu Jitsu: a propensity for ground control and the ability to bring an unwilling opponent into that very sphere by take-down, sweep or otherwise.

Fig 15.0 has uke attacking with the typical two-handed collar clinch, an expected and ever-predictable attack of the common variety.

Fig 15.0

Fig 15.1 Tori uses any number of escapes to break the collar hold (but could also operate despite it) and immediately steps perpendicular to uke, the left foot having stepped across uke's front and now nearly touching uke's left. Tori is turning his hip into uke and beginning to maneuver his nearest arm under uke's arm on the same side, preparing to wrap that arm about uke in the direction the arrow is pointing.

Fig 15.1

Fig 15.2 Tori has dropped his hips more here. As he's taller than his attacker and has a naturally higher center of gravity he'll have to dip that much more to get his hips lower to the floor than his opponent's for the lifting process to work correctly and efficiently. Tori's near arm can be seen to have gotten below uke's and is now proceeding to wrap and secure about the torso of uke for the lifting action (as indicated by the upper arrow). The lower arrow points to where tori will bring his foot prior to making the lift.

Fig 15.2

Fig 15.3 As soon as tori senses his hip placement is low enough and is below his attacker's, his securement arm firmly clasps uke to him (circling arrow), his near side arm maintains a clinch on either uke's wrist or the clothes covering his arm, and he begins to straighten his bent knees. This process is accompanied by tori pulling uke towards him with his hugging arm, while the near arm pulls uke in the same direction to the front of tori. All of this will come together most dramatically when uke's feet leave the floor (upper arrow) and leverage begins to pull him forwards.

Fig 15.3

Fig 15.4 Tori has created the leveraging force necessary to pull uke forward with his far arm (seen here holding uke's wrist). It is the use of his hip as a fulcrum however, that makes the throw so powerful and practicable, and doesn't require that tori lift uke off the floor any more than a little to accomplish the throw. Tori controls the trajectory of the attacker with the hugging arm and guides him along the curved path of the downward arrow.

Fig 15.4

Fig 15.5 Uke falls rapidly in the direction tori intends and the arrow points, with all control over his speed and direction in the hands of his opponent.

Fig 15.5

Fig 15.6 Uke lands, rattled and shaken, as tori prepares to execute the next phase of his counter-attack, that which will be actuated using the arm he's still holding. From here tori needs only to step over uke's fallen form with one leg in the direction of the arrow and he can begin the bone lock, or kansetsu waza.

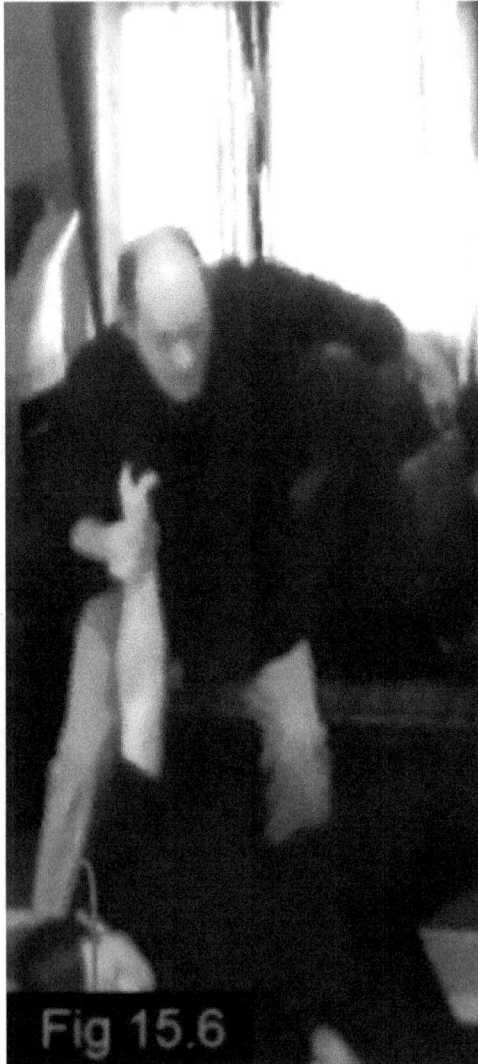

Fig 15.6

Fig 15.7 After having stepped over uke with his right leg, tori allows himself to roll back onto his back, and then places his remaining leg across uke's torso to effectively create a control on the other's ability to move (indicated by the dotted lines). Tori, holding the end of uke's arm, needs now only fall back to accomplish the bone lock.

Fig 15.7

Fig 15.8 Tori uses his hip to apply upward pressure to uke's locked arm, similar to the force generated when using a fulcrum, so that enough force applied below it can overtax the elbow joint in direct line with the hip, and by doing so break it. That force is indicated by the upward arrow, while towards the face of tori the downward arrow makes clear the clutching and securing force being exerted against the end of uke's arm to deny it space to flex or escape.

Fig 15.8

Within the foregoing pages the writer has tried to impart a sense of the essence of Jūjutsu to the reader, be it Brazilian Jiu Jitsu, Japanese Aiki-Jūjutsu or Japanese Jūjutsu along with a sense of the rationale and mentality that belongs to the methodology by which the martial sciences operate. While providing but a fractional glimpse into these processes and practices, the writer hopes the reader comes away with an increased understanding of Jūjutsu and an appreciation of its history, as well as insights into the mechanics and dynamics of the martial arts in general, even be it only proportional to the length and depth of the work itself. On this subject a great many powerful practitioners and authors and historians exist that have created written works far more substantial than that found here, and it would be to the reader's benefit to seek those works out and give them due consideration.

About the Author

D.S. Hopkins has been a practitioner of Jūjutsu for over twenty years, holds the rank of Shodan and has instructed others in it as well as practiced disciplines outside of it. He has been a writer longer than that which he's been a martial artist, pursuing expertise in genres outside of non-fiction.

Endnotes

1   Shiro Omiya, The Hidden Roots of Aikido, Aiki-Jūjutsu Daito-Ryu (Tokyo: Kodansha International, Ltd. 1998) 15-16.
2   Shiro Omiya, The Hidden Roots of Aikido, Aiki-Jūjutsu Daito-Ryu (Tokyo: Kodansha International, Ltd. 1998) 15-16.
3   Stephen R. Turnbull, The Book of the Samurai, The Warrior Class Of Japan (Wigston: Magna Books, 1987), 125.
4   Grzegorz Zabinski, Bartlomiej Walczak, and Codex Wallerstein, A Medieval Fighting Book from the Fifteenth Century on the Longsword, Falchion, Dagger and Wrestling (Boulder: Paladin Press, 2002), 73 - 91, 141 - 305, 354 – 357.
5   Stephen R. Turnbull, The Lone Samurai and the Martial Arts (London: Arms and Armour Press, 1990), 92.
6   Actual experience of this writer; counter move against forward strangle attempt.
7   To this very day I'm not actually sure what the video was of, a tournament such as PRIDE FC, UFC or something else; and the professed expertise exceeded four disciplines.
8   ARMA, The Association For Renaissance Martial Arts.
9   This writer has personally experienced such a precision attack on a vital point, at the outset of martial art training in a Jūjutsu system of fight during the mid 90s: a chop, six inches away, to the jugular. The effect is described here accurately.
10   I've actually experienced this multiple times during my younger years, and all of the disappointment that comes with it.
11   "Violent Crimes by Characteristics of Incident," U.S. Census Bureau, 2010, accessed January 03, 2015,
http://www.census.gov/compendia/statab/2012/tables/12s0317.pdf
12   "Uniform Crime Reports, 2012 Law Enforcement Officers Killed & Assaulted," Department of Justice, Federal Bureau Of Investigation, last accessed January 03, 2015,
    http://www.fbi.gov/about-us/cjis/ucr/leoka/2012/tables/table_70_leos_asltd_type_of_weapon_and_percent_injured_2003-2012.xls
13   "Uniform Crime Reports, Crime in the United States 2013," U.S. Department of Justice - Federal Bureau of Investigation, last accessed January 03, 2015,
http://www.fbi.gov/about-us/cjis/ucr/crime-in-the-u.s/2013/crime-in-the-u.s.-2013/tables/table-19/table_19_rate_additional_information_about_selected_offenses_by_population_group_2013.xls
    "Uniform Crime Reports, Crime in the United States 2012," U.S. Department

of Justice - Federal Bureau of Investigation, last accessed January 03, 2015,
http://www.fbi.gov/about-us/cjis/ucr/crime-in-the-u.s/2012/crime-in-the-u.s.-
2012/tables/19tabledatadecpdf/table_19_rate_by_selected_offenses_2012.xls

"Uniform Crime Reports, Crime in the United States 2011, Violent Crime,
Aggravated Assault" U.S. Department of Justice - Federal Bureau of Investigation,
last accessed January 03, 2015, http://www.fbi.gov/about-us/cjis/ucr/crime-in-the-
u.s/2011/crime-in-the-u.s.-2011/violent-crime/aggravated-assault

"Uniform Crime Reports, Crime in the United States 2010," U.S. Department
of Justice - Federal Bureau of Investigation, last accessed January 03, 2015,
http://www.fbi.gov/about-us/cjis/ucr/crime-in-the-u.s/2010/crime-in-the-u.s.-
2010/tables/10tbl19.xls

"Uniform Crime Reports, Crime in the United States 2009," U.S. Department
of Justice - Federal Bureau of Investigation, last accessed January 03, 2015,
http://www2.fbi.gov/ucr/cius2009/data/table_19.html

"Uniform Crime Reports, Crime in the United States 2008," U.S. Department
of Justice - Federal Bureau of Investigation, last accessed January 03, 2015,
http://www2.fbi.gov/ucr/cius2008/data/table_19.html

"Uniform Crime Reports, Crime in the United States 2007," U.S. Department
of Justice - Federal Bureau of Investigation, last accessed January 03, 2015,
http://www2.fbi.gov/ucr/cius2007/data/table_19.html

14   "Uniform Crime Reports, Crime in the United States 2013," U.S. Department
of Justice - Federal Bureau of Investigation, last accessed January 03, 2015,
http://www.fbi.gov/about-us/cjis/ucr/crime-in-the-u.s/2013/crime-in-the-u.s.-
2013/tables/table-
19/table_19_rate_additional_information_about_selected_offenses_by_population_g
roup_2013.xls

"Uniform Crime Reports, Crime in the United States 2012," U.S. Department
of Justice - Federal Bureau of Investigation, last accessed January 03, 2015,
http://www.fbi.gov/about-us/cjis/ucr/crime-in-the-u.s/2012/crime-in-the-u.s.-
2012/tables/19tabledatadecpdf/table_19_rate_by_selected_offenses_2012.xls

"Uniform Crime Reports, Crime in the United States 2011, Violent Crime,
Aggravated Assault" U.S. Department of Justice - Federal Bureau of Investigation,
last accessed January 03, 2015, http://www.fbi.gov/about-us/cjis/ucr/crime-in-the-
u.s/2011/crime-in-the-u.s.-2011/violent-crime/aggravated-assault

"Uniform Crime Reports, Crime in the United States 2010" U.S. Department of
Justice - Federal Bureau of Investigation, last accessed January 03, 2015,
http://www.fbi.gov/about-us/cjis/ucr/crime-in-the-u.s/2010/crime-in-the-u.s.-
2010/tables/10tbl19.xls

"Uniform Crime Reports, Crime in the United States 2009," U.S. Department
of Justice - Federal Bureau of Investigation, last accessed January 03, 2015,
http://www2.fbi.gov/ucr/cius2009/data/table_19.html

"Uniform Crime Reports, Crime in the United States 2008" U.S. Department of
Justice - Federal Bureau of Investigation, last accessed January 03, 2015,
http://www2.fbi.gov/ucr/cius2008/data/table_19.html

"Uniform Crime Reports, Crime in the United States 2007" U.S. Department of
Justice - Federal Bureau of Investigation, last accessed January 03, 2015,

http://www2.fbi.gov/ucr/cius2007/data/table_19.html
15   □ Terry Glavin,"Cougar Attack," Canadian Geographic, May/June 2004: 53 – 66.

www.ingramcontent.com/pod-product-compliance
Lightning Source LLC
LaVergne TN
LVHW051504080426
835509LV00017B/1910